I0752746

IMAGES
of America

KIRTLAND AIR FORCE BASE

ON THE COVER: A B-50 crew from the 4925th Test Group (Atomic) readies for a mission. (Courtesy of the Air Force Nuclear Weapons Center History Office.)

IMAGES
of America

KIRTLAND AIR FORCE BASE

Joseph T. Page II

ARCADIA
PUBLISHING

ISBN 9781540235114

Published by Arcadia Publishing
Charleston, South Carolina

Library of Congress Control Number: 2018941671

For all general information, please contact Arcadia Publishing:
Telephone 843-853-2070
Fax 843-853-0044
E-mail sales@arcadiapublishing.com
For customer service and orders:
Toll-Free 1-888-313-2665

Visit us on the Internet at www.arcadiapublishing.com

This book is dedicated to Adam Paul Burma (US Navy). When the call "Whom shall I send? And who will go for us?" came, Adam stood and said, "Here am I. Send me!" (Author's collection.)

Contents

Acknowledgments

First, I owe thanks to James "Al" Moyers, historian for the Air Force Nuclear Weapons Center. Al provided a large amount of unclassified photographs on the history of Kirtland. What I am most grateful for was his patience in explaining the nuances of how the base began and later formed to its present-day size.

Thanks to Matt Thompson, resident "additional duty" historian at the Defense Nuclear Weapons School. By happenstance, our paths crossed and Matt provided invaluable suggestions and referential material. This book would not have been completed if not for Matt's assistance.

Steve Watson, an archivist with the Air Force History and Museums program, was kind enough to write the introduction for chapter one. He is *the* expert on Colonel Kirtland's life. I hope to see an in-depth biography on Kirtland (the man) soon.

Additional thanks to Dr. Circe Woessner, Valkyrie, Martin "@NuclearAnthro" Pfeiffer, Dave Reynolds, Bruce Rose, Laura Malloy, Sue Fye, Blackjack, Jennifer Hayden, Jerry Little, the Albuquerque Public Library system, Shadow, and the 377th Air Base Wing Public Affairs Office.

Special kudos go to Ben Wash for sharing his tales of B-52 alert duty in the waning days of the Cold War, and Jeremy "J.J." Jackson, for being a "Jack of All Trades" and the best NCO anyone could ask for.

Perpetual gratitude to Satellite Coffee baristas Avery, Marcus, Genevieve, Marissa, Gabby, Tia, Daniel, Benji, Sam, Billy, and Katelin. Props to Starbucks baristas Celestina, Jacob, and Maximo.

Special thanks to my parents, Joe and Kathy, for bringing our family to New Mexico. I became acquainted with Kirtland in the 1990s when my father attended Air Force Systems Command's Non-Commissioned Officer Academy on base. (Lab Ducks, indeed!)

Finally, a loving thanks to my soulmate, Kim, and our (wild) tribe of children. I hope they will find New Mexico home as I did, a transplant from far-off places enamored with the Land of Enchantment's endless blue skies.

Unless otherwise noted, all images were provided by the United States Air Force.

The selection of photographs and coverage of people, places, and weapons and any subsequent errors of omission or commission are solely the author's fault.

Introduction

Named for an airman who had no connection to the base or its location, Kirtland Air Force Base is arguably more a national center for research and development, acquisition and sustainment, testing and evaluation, and combat training and readiness, than it is a traditional Air Force base with combat-ready squadrons. Occupying a large military reservation adjacent to Albuquerque, New Mexico, the base's presence is significant to the local economic and social life. Much of Kirtland's history has been involved with military aviation since the years immediately preceding World War II. The war years led directly to the installation's present status as one of the nation's most important defense facilities.

Prewar Aviation

Private and commercial aviation began during and after World War I at landing sites on the open East Mesa. Military flyers began using the early airfield at Albuquerque (named Oxnard Field after its owner James Oxnard) as a convenient stop during coast-to-coast flights. With the Albuquerque Municipal Airport in planning stages by 1937, many business and civic leaders who promoted the new facility thought military aviation activity would also benefit the city.

The outbreak of war in Europe helped further the cause for military aviation in Albuquerque. In late 1939, the US Army Air Corps leased 2,000 acres adjacent to the municipal airport from the city. This location housed a small detachment to service transient Army and Navy aircraft until construction began on Albuquerque Army Air Base on January 7, 1941, months before the bombing of Pearl Harbor. The initial base construction was completed in early August 1941. The first construction projects were aimed at housing and supplying the 19th Bombardment Group and its attached support units. In addition, the existing 5,000-foot, north-south runway was lengthened to accommodate Boeing B-17 Flying Fortress bombers.

The flying units of the 19th Bombardment Group transferred from March Field, California, to Albuquerque in the summer of 1941 even before base construction was completed. Commanding this bomber organization was Lt. Col. Eugene L. Eubank, for whom Albuquerque's Eubank Boulevard is named. Colonel Eubank demanded his pilots have extensive cockpit experience, receiving training as navigators and bombardiers. This would pay dividends when the unit became engaged in the Pacific theater of war.

The group transferred locations to train its flight crews and support personnel for reconnaissance and bombing duties. Assigned to fly the B-17, which was in short supply in 1941, the group trained on Douglas B-18 and Northrup A-17 aircraft, as well as Stearman PT-17 biplanes until they received their full complement of B-17s.

To provide transition training for four-engine aircraft, Army Air Corps leadership selected Trans World Airlines (TWA) and their large Albuquerque presence. The training facility was officially titled the Air Corps Ferrying Command Four-Engine Transition School. However, it was unofficially referred to as the "Four-Engine School" or the "Jack Frye School," after the president of TWA. The location of the Four-Engine School was also unofficially called the "Eagle Nest Flight Center." The Army Air Corps Ferrying Command operated the school, which was organized to transport aircraft to the British Royal Air Force. Students trained on Consolidated B-24 bombers and other multi-engine aircraft in use by the Royal Air Force. The first group of trainees arrived in June 1941, around the time the Army Air Corps became the US Army Air Forces, reflecting the increased importance of military aviation preparations. In July 1942, the Four-Engine School was transferred to Tennessee.

World War II

In October 1941, with reassignment of the 19th Bombardment Group to the Pacific, Army Air Forces leadership decided to move the Barksdale Field bombardier school from Louisiana to New Mexico. Decision factors included ideal flying weather and large vacant tracts of land available for use as bombing ranges. The bombardier school was designated the Air Forces Advanced Flying School, Albuquerque Army Air Base, New Mexico, commanded by Col. Frank D. Hackett. The school officially activated on December 24, 1941, days after the United States officially entered World War II.

Training Schools

The bombardier school at Kirtland Field was the most important and continuous activity during the duration of World War II. The first class of bombardiers graduated on March 7, 1942. By 1945, the school had trained 5,719 bombardier students.

The Glider Replacement Center operated at Kirtland Field in 1942 and 1943. The first glider students arrived on July 8, 1942, starting fitness training in preparation for training. In February 1943, however, the whole glider training program was reorganized and the Kirtland glider school was closed. Glider students transferred to other military specialties or to aviation cadet schools.

On August 1, 1943, the Army Air Forces established a B-24 Pilot Transition School at Kirtland to train students in the operation of the B-24 to qualify them to become aircraft commanders. A bombardier pilot school was also established to train bomber pilots and bombardiers in techniques for weapons delivery. By early 1945, Kirtland Field trained over 1,750 pilots and crew members for the B-24 bomber alone. During February 1945, combat crew training for the Boeing B-29 Superfortress began at Albuquerque and continued until the end of the war.

At the end of World War II, Kirtland's future was unknown. The civilian and military workforce declined drastically, and for two months, the base was placed in standby status until a postwar mission was determined. Transferred to Strategic Air Command on March 1, 1945, Kirtland Field was inactivated, then again transferred to the Fourth Air Force and subsequently to the Fifteenth Air Force. Events of 1946, however, resurrected Kirtland Field as an important installation. World events, such as the atomic tests during Operation Crossroads, indicated a need for support bases for aircraft taking place in similar atomic (and later nuclear) tests. Kirtland Field was ultimately reactivated on December 1, 1946, as an installation of the Army Air Force's Air Materiel Command.

Sandia Base

Entering World War II, the Army Air Forces had a critical need for trained aircraft mechanics and air depot service personnel. Officials established a training center for such personnel near Albuquerque, taking approximately 1,100 acres of land adjacent to the eastern edge of Kirtland Field. During May 1942, the Albuquerque Air Depot Training Station (unofficially referred to as Sandia Base), opened and became a facility of the Air Service Command of the Army Air Forces.

By June 1, 1942, the Air Depot Training Station held over 2,300 officers and enlisted men stationed as either instructors or students. By October 1943, four air base groups had been trained at the station and sent overseas to provide depot-level maintenance. Midway through the war, the Army had less need for similar groups. Consequently, the Air Depot Training Station became the Albuquerque Army Air Field when the last depot contingent departed.

By mid-1944, the field found new life as the Army Air Forces Convalescent Center. Barracks and support facilities were used to house wounded air crewmen who were recovering from surgery or requiring other medical services. Old depot facilities were reused to provide space for essential services and occupational therapy for over 800 convalescent airmen, in addition to a rest and recreation facility. The convalescent center closed in April 1945 as the need for its services dwindled, reverting again to an Army air field.

As World War II came to an end, the air field began receiving the first of some 2,250 surplus military aircraft. By late 1945, rows of B-17, B-24, and B-29 bombers awaited disposal by the Reconstruction Finance Corporation (later the War Assets Administration) at Albuquerque Army Air Field.

During September 1945, Los Alamos's Z Division (named for its chief, Dr. Jerrold Zacharias) moved to Oxnard Field. The Manhattan Engineer District authorized construction of guard, storage, administrative, and laboratory facilities for the newly designated Sandia Base. The location later became the home of the Sandia Corporation, and today's Sandia National Laboratories.

Defense Nuclear Weapons School

On January 1, 1947, the Armed Forces Special Weapons Project was activated with its field headquarters at Sandia Base to replace the Manhattan Engineer District's role in the nation's atomic energy program. General Groves, former Manhattan Engineer District head, organized the Armed Forces Special Weapons Project (AFSWP) for directing military efforts associated with development of atomic weapons as an inter-service organization reporting directly to the War Department.

Under AFSWP, the Technical Training Group trained weapons technicians for assembly and repair of early atomic bombs. Changes in names also brought changes in mission, with the Special Weapons Training Group teaching accident response, production bomb designs, and nuclear explosive ordnance disposal.

As the pace of special weapons development quickened, the Department of Defense created the Defense Atomic Support Agency in May 1959 to supersede the AFSWP. The organization was renamed in 1971 to the Defense Nuclear Agency, with increasing scope for stockpile management, testing, and weapons effects research programs. The current incarnation of the institution under the Defense Threat Reduction Agency—the Defense Nuclear Weapons School—maintains an impressive legacy of the instructing stewards of the nuclear weapons enterprise for over seven decades.

Manzano Base

In 1948, the US Army's Albuquerque District received $10 million to build a weapons storage facility directly east of Kirtland. Manzano Base was considered a separate, self-contained installation, relying on Sandia Base for logistics support. As time went on, however, Sandia Base organizations took over more support functions for Manzano. The base essentially became the Manzano area of Sandia Base until the consolidation of the three bases in 1971.

Naval Weapons Evaluation Facility

The Naval Weapons Evaluation Facility was part of the Naval Air Systems Command, providing test and evaluation for nuclear and nonnuclear weapons systems. First formed in 1948 at Kirtland Field, the unit quickly grew to become the Naval Air Special Weapons Facility in 1952, and the Naval Weapons Evaluation Facility (NWEF) in 1961. NWEF was involved in the compatibility and safety certification of over 32 different types of aircraft in the US Navy inventory before its inactivation in 1993.

New Mexico Air National Guard

Kirtland has hosted New Mexico's component of the Air National Guard since 1947. Federally recognized as the 188th Fighter Bomber Squadron on July 7, 1947, the unit flew Martin B-26 bombers and North American F-51 fighters in its early years. In the early 1970s, the 150th took over a new role, along with a new jet. In 1974, the group received the Vought A-7D, a close air support jet. After a period of flying the F-16 in the late 1990s and early 2000s, the 150th changed missions once again, to become a special operations wing through Total Force Integration and cooperation with the 58th Special Operations Wing.

Air Force Research Laboratory

On May 1, 1963, the Air Force Weapons Laboratory was established at Kirtland from elements of the Air Force Special Weapons Center to engage in weapons research and development of simulation techniques, since atmospheric, space, or underwater testing was no longer possible. In 1982, the Air Force Space Technology Center activated at Kirtland to become the focal point for technology planning and development for Air Force space missions. In 1990, officials redesignated the Air Force Space Technology Center as the Phillips Laboratory. By 1997, Phillips Laboratory was inactivated as its components were reorganized into the Air Force Research Laboratory structure, with two directorates: the Space Vehicles Directorate, and the Directed Energy Directorate.

Pararescue Training

Drawing upon the experience of combat search and rescue in Southeast Asia, the Air Mobility Command activated the 1550th Aircrew Training and Test Wing at Hill Air Force Base, Utah, on April 1, 1971, to serve as a test center and school for rescue aircrews and technology. The wing moved to Kirtland Air Force Base on February 20, 1976, and continued training helicopter and fixed-wing aircrews. Pararescue training continues today under the aegis of the 58th Special Operations Wing and its squadrons.

Air Force Nuclear Weapons Center

Created in 2006, the Air Force Nuclear Weapons Center (AFNWC) is the descendant organization of the Air Force Special Weapons Center. Its directorates oversee the various aspects of nuclear materiel management. Today, AFNWC controls the base host unit, the 377th Air Base Wing, and reports to the Air Force Global Strike Command.

Golden Legacy, Limitless Future

This brief introduction, and the collection of photographs to follow, only scratch the surface of an amazing history of the hundreds of organizations that have called Kirtland AFB home. Over time, many of the administrative functions—security, fire protection, communications, and civil engineering—have been consolidated, while other organizations, such as air defense and radar sites, have disappeared entirely. The sheer number of units and their individual histories preclude comprehensive coverage within this book. These organizations and their legacies comprise the distinctive partnership that is presently known as Kirtland Air Force Base.

One

Roy Carrington Kirtland

Roy Carrington Kirtland will be remembered as a pioneer of American military aviation. Born into an Army family at Fort Benton, Montana, on May 14, 1874, he enlisted in the Army infantry in 1898. Rising quickly through the enlisted ranks, he was promoted to first lieutenant in 1901 and participated in the Philippines Insurrection. Something of an adventurer, Kirtland discovered photography, kayaking, and motorcycling.

In March 1911, Kirtland was recruited into aviation, then controlled by the Signal Corps, which needed officers from other branches to fill its aviation needs. Kirtland was sent to the Aviation School in College Park, Maryland, and obtained his pilot's license later that year. The handful of young pilots there were among the world's first aviators, and experimented in night landings, firing machine guns and dropping bombs, and radio communications.

But the safety of early aircraft was problematic, and there was no means for advancement within aviation for non–Signal Corps pilots. Kirtland and others rebelled against these issues, first in 1912–1913, and later in 1916 in the Goodier court martial. But their efforts were overshadowed by the Punitive Expedition and World War I.

During the First World War, Kirtland commanded a motor mechanics regiment sent to France, and then inspected aviation rest camps in England. After the war, he oversaw repair depots before being sent to Army schools, first as a student and then as an instructor, and then to the prestigious Army War College. Kirtland became the Army Air Corps personnel representative on the Army General Staff, then commanded Langley Field, Virginia, and went on to become a liaison officer between aviators and ground troops. Colonel Kirtland would end his career as an Air Corps inspector, retiring in 1938 to Coronado, California.

But in the buildup to World War II, Kirtland returned to active duty in April 1941, only to die of a heart condition three weeks later, on May 2, 1941. Maj. Gen. Henry "Hap" Arnold, commander of the Army Air Forces, was instrumental in the naming of Albuquerque Army Airfield in honor of his old friend Roy Kirtland.

USA

WAR DEPARTMENT WASHINGTON, D. C.

THIS IS TO CERTIFY THAT

Roy C. Kirtland,

FIRST LIEUT. 14TH INFANTRY,

IS RATED AS A

MILITARY AVIATOR

from the seventeenth day of January 1913. upon which date he successfully completed the tests prescribed by the War Department and that notation to that effect has been made on his record.

ACTING SECRETARY OF WAR.

CHIEF SIGNAL OFFICER

COMMANDING SIGNAL CORPS AVIATION SCHOOL

Recorded in the Office of The Adjutant General

THE ADJUTANT GENERAL

August 19. 1913.

1st Lt. Roy C. Kirtland earned his military aviation certificate on January 17, 1913. As one of the earliest Army pilots, Kirtland's aviation expertise was recognized with certificate No. 45 from the Federation Aeronautique Internationale (1911) and expert aviator license No. 11 from the Aero Club of America. (Courtesy of Steve Watson.)

Lieutenant Kirtland poses on a Wright Model B at College Park, Maryland, in 1911. On March 28, 1911, he was ordered into aviation and his initial task was to oversee construction of four hangars at College Park. He held the post of school secretary in addition to serving as a flying instructor.

From left to right, Capt. Paul Beck, Lt. H.H. Arnold, Capt. C.F. Chandler, Lt. T.D. Milling, and Lt. Roy Kirtland pose in front of a Wright Flyer at College Park in July 1911. Arnold would later rise to command the Air Corps, then become chief of the Army Air Forces in 1941, and finally the Air Force's only five-star general in 1949. (Courtesy of the Air Force Historical Research Agency.)

On June 7, 1912, Lieutenant Kirtland (right) is pictured in the pilot's seat of a Wright Model B in College Park, with Capt. Charles deForest Chandler, commander of the US Army flying school. This staged photo was intended to depict the first firing of a machine gun from an aircraft; however, the actual pilot, Lieutenant Milling, was absent that day and Kirtland sat in for him. The Lewis gun was an air-cooled, gas-operated, magazine-fed light machine gun, with a fire rate of 500–600 rounds per minute.

Early US Army aviators pose at College Park in 1911. From left to right are (first row) Lt. Louis C. Rockwell and Lt. Thomas D. Milling; (second row) Capt. Hennessy, Lt. H.H. Arnold, Lt. Roy C. Kirtland, Capt. Frank N, Kennedy, Lt. McLeary, and Lt. Harold Geiger. Arnold, Kirtland, Milling, McLeary, and Geiger were among the original 24 military aviators. Rockwell was later killed, while Kennedy and Hennessey left aviation before completing their licenses.

This photograph contains the core of the First Aero Squadron–Provisional, organized on March 5, 1913. As the US military's oldest flying unit, the squadron has seen action in every major conflict from the Punitive Expedition through the Global War on Terror. Lieutenant Kirtland (second row center) was the squadron adjutant and supply officer, under the command of Captain Cowan, seated in front of him.

In this official photograph of Col. Roy Carrington Kirtland, below his ribbon rack he wears the original Military Aviator insignia given to the first 24 Army aviators, depicting an eagle with the Signal Corps flags in its talons, suspended from a bar embossed with "Military Aviator." Kirtland's final assignment was at the West Coast Army Air Forces Training Center, Moffett Field, California. Arriving in April 1941, he suffered a fatal heart attack shortly thereafter.

WAR DEPARTMENT

HEADQUARTERS OF THE ARMY AIR FORCES

WASHINGTON

FEB 19 1942

Mrs. Roy C. Kirtland,
901 "A" Avenue,
Coronado, California.

My dear Helen:

Knowing Roy for so many years and taking full cognizance of his early flying and his work on aircraft development, I was desirous of initiating action toward a permanent recognition of his distinguished service to the nation. It pleases me, therefore, very greatly to advise that the large new army flying field at Albuquerque, New Mexico has been named in his honor, "Kirtland Field".

The simple "official announcement" inclosed was issued as the orders of the Secretary of War and I am sending you a copy as I know you will be glad to have it. The War Department, in its recognition thus perpetuates Roy's name throughout the service and the country. I know that you will feel that such recognition is deservedly placed.

With kindest personal regards,

Sincerely yours,

H. H. Arnold

H. H. ARNOLD
Lieutenant General, U.S.A.
Chief of the Army Air Forces.

Incl.
AGO ltr. 2-6-42.

Lt. Gen. Henry Arnold, chief of the Army Air Forces, sent this letter to Colonel Kirtland's widow, Helen, informing her of the renaming of Albuquerque Army Air Base to Kirtland Field in 1942.

Two

World War to Cold War, 1941–1959

The Second World War (1939–1945) saw the world's great powers forming two opposing military alliances: the Allies and the Axis. The United States was officially drawn into the conflict on December 7, 1941, following the Japanese attack on US forces in the Pacific. During the length of the war, Albuquerque held a few of the most critical activities for the aerial war effort: bombardier and navigation training, four-engine transition school, glider training, aviation maintenance, and convalescent center for returning aircrews. Support to the Manhattan Project came during the later war years.

Testing for another vital war project, the proximity fuse, was conducted on the New Mexico Proving Grounds: 50,000 acres of land stretching from the southern end of the Manzano Mountains to the Isleta Pueblo. These fuses helped counteract the devastating German V-1 attacks on London and were dubbed "the second most important weapon" developed during World War II.

In 1946, the Manhattan Engineering District was closed down, replaced by the Atomic Energy Commission, a civilian-run organization. To interact with the AEC, the War Department created the Armed Forces Special Weapons Project (AFSWP). The Air Force's portion of the AFSWP was the Air Force Special Weapons Command, later renamed the Air Force Special Weapons Center. AFSWC exercised operational control of all aircraft during select atmospheric nuclear tests, while providing air support to supervising Joint Task Forces. Aircraft and crews were based out of Indian Springs, an airfield 24 miles southeast of the Nevada Test Site. In a few select missions, such as shot WASP during Operation Teapot, 4950th Test Group aircrews would airdrop the weapons during the tests.

The air defense mission began at Kirtland in 1948 but was reassigned to the Albuquerque Air Defense Sector in 1950. After a brief period, the air defense sector was inactivated and the mission was assigned to the 34th Air Division.

The runway from Oxnard Field stretches eastward toward Tijeras Canyon and the Manzano Mountains. Originating from Frank Speakman and William Franklin's 1928 partnership, and the sponsorship of Albuquerque mayor Clyde Tingley, the Albuquerque airport was built on 140 acres on the East Mesa and later acquired by James Oxnard. Purchase of the field by the US Army in April 1942 restricted the field to military use only. The air terminal location is now the site of the Sandia Area Federal Credit Union.

The first troops arrive at the Albuquerque railway station in December 1941, waiting for transport to Albuquerque Army Air Base. Base construction began nearly a year before, but after the Pearl Harbor attack, the need to train aircrews grew significantly.

The Waco CG-4A combat glider, known as the Flying Coffin, flew at the Glider Replacement School from 1942 to 1943. The aircraft was little more than a fabric-covered wood and metal frame, crewed by a pilot and copilot. CG-4s could carry 13 passengers, or one Jeep and four passengers. Considered expendable, after landing they would be abandoned or destroyed by allied personnel.

A Beech AT-11 Kansan flies over West Texas. AT-11s were used for bombardier training at Kirtland and other airfields around the state. The aircraft had a glass-encased bombardier station built into the nose, mirroring the design of the B-17, B-24, and B-29 bombers. Over 1,500 AT-11s were ordered for the US Army Air Forces. (Courtesy of Air Force Historical Research Agency.)

Bombardier students walk past a B-18 bomber. The Douglas B-18 Bolo was a medium bomber serving in the Army Air Corps from the late 1930s to the early 1940s. Lt. Sid Young flew the first B-18 Bolo into Albuquerque Army Air Base on April 1, 1941, initiating the flying mission of the nascent base.

B-24 Liberators fly in formation over New Mexico. Early training with B-24s concentrated on ferry missions to deliver aircraft to Great Britain. The first B-24 students arrived in Albuquerque in June 1941, at the Air Corps Ferrying Command Four-Engine Transition School. Unofficially, however, the school was known as the Jack Frye School at the Eagle's Nest Flight Center.

This is a c. 1943 high-altitude aerial view of Kirtland Field. Training aircraft crowd the field's parking ramps.

An American Legion convention tour group poses in front of a B-24 in 1942. Support for the war effort depended on War Bond drives orchestrated by groups such as the Legion. Tours such as this gave members a brief glimpse into the lives of the young men and women at Kirtland preparing for war.

An unidentified man and woman perform parachute rigging duties, inspecting for any damage, tears, or fraying. As part of an aircrew's flying gear, this critical piece of equipment understandably meant the difference between life and death during a bailout.

From: The BOMBSIGHT, KIRTLAND FIELD, NM ARMY AIR FORCES ADVANCED FLYING SCHOOL NEWS LETTER 1 JUNE, 1943

"BOMBARDIER"

SCENES FAMILIAR to every GI stationed here at Kirtland are being flashed on the screens throughout America in the picture, "Bombardier". Hangers, barracks and the surrounding mountains are to be seen in the picture. At the initial showing here in Albuquerque, some fortunate GIs saw themselves in action shots taken here on the Field.

"Bombardier" will give the "folks back home" an opportunity to see where their sons and daughters are training and working, and they will see classroom scenes, in the actual classroom, that were filmed showing the actual equipment used in training bombardiers for their important job.

The picture portrays the life and training of bombardier cadets at Kirtland Field...And their ultimate goal, Tokyo. Combining thrilling flight scenes with a touch of romance, the picture never drags, hold audiences spellbound.

12

A June 1943 article in *The Bombsight*, the Advanced Flying School newsletter, describes the filming of *Bombardier* at the airfield. Kirtland Field hosted Hollywood filmmakers for six weeks in late 1942. The motion picture starred Pat O'Brien and Randolph Scott and showed the life of two competing pilots during World War II. The film was well received by the public and was nominated for an Academy Award for special effects.

Actress Anne Shirley (1918–1993), the female lead in *Bombardier*, sits during a break in filming. Born Dawn O'Day, Shirley took her stage name from Lucy Maud Montgomery's literary heroine. She retired from acting in 1944, at the age of 26, one year after *Bombardier* was released.

A film crew records a scene from *Bombardier*. The movie premiered on May 14, 1943, and was screened at Kirtland. The tradition of commercial filming at Kirtland, initiated by *Bombardier*, continues into the present day with many blockbuster movies.

Students pose for a class photograph on the steps of the Bombardier Ground School. By 1945, the bombardier school had graduated over 5,700 bombardiers just for the B-24 fleet. The school ranged from 12 to 18 weeks, where precise records tallied a student's hits and misses.

A bombardier trainee takes an oath, with his hand on his charge, to guard the bombsight to ensure its technology did not fall into enemy hands. Contrary to popular myths surrounding the Norden bombsight, its promise of accurate bomb delivery depended on near-perfect conditions, unlikely in wartime.

A bombardier trainee is evaluated by an instructor in a B-17 mockup. Before trainees were allowed anywhere near an operational aircraft, prudence demanded many hours of ground school to practice fundamentals. Trainees learned to balance the many factors of accurate bombing techniques, to include optical principles, direction, speed, movement, weather, and enemy response, to name a few.

The Sandia Mountains fill a bombardier's view from the cockpit. Albuquerque's population hovered around 35,449 in 1940. Positive selection factors for bombardment training, such as sparse population and clear flying weather, are easily seen from this image.

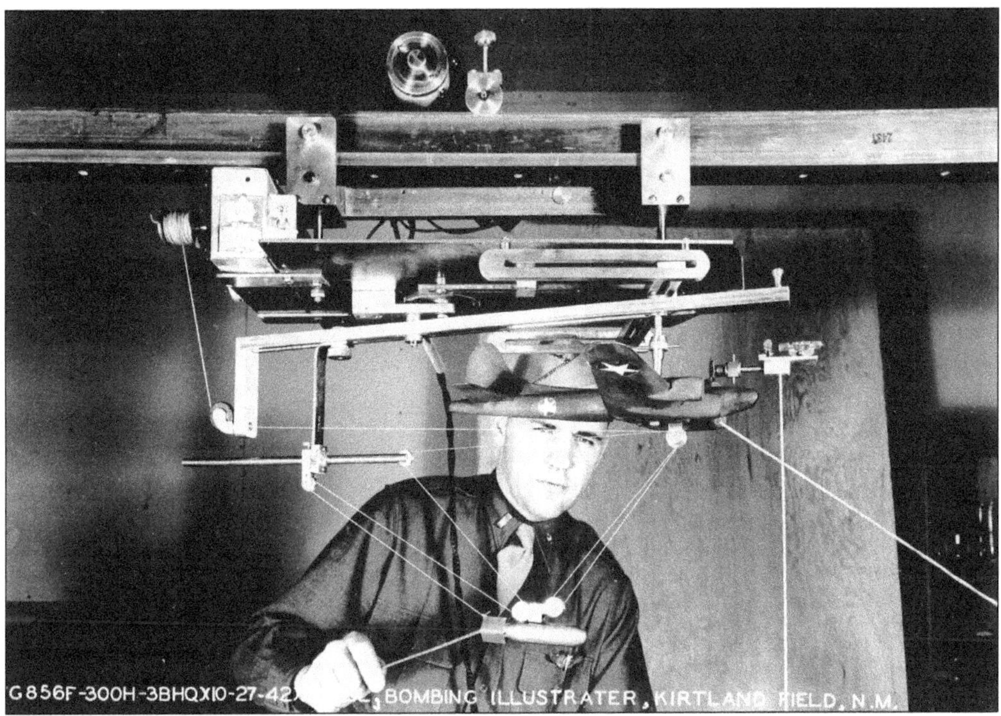

An instructor (above), demonstrates the physics of a bomb drop using a wire-and-pulley "bombing illustrater," while below, students investigate a simulated drop on a model tank. Analog computers, such as the bombsight, helped determine the precise drop time and distance for an accurate strike. Bombardment skills were critical in combat; a flying squadron would often synchronize their bomb release off the formation's lead aircraft. An early release would mean a failed strike and likely a repeat mission in the future.

Sgt. George Skamanich poses under the 88th School Squadron sign. A flight engineer on B-24s, Skamanich was stationed at Kirtland for the duration of the war since he had three brothers serving in combat. He later served in Korea on C-46 Commando transports. (Courtesy of the Skamanich family.)

B-24s are pictured flying over the Sandia Mountains. Compared to the B-17 Flying Fortress, the Liberator had a longer range and higher top speed. These advantages, however, were negated by a higher accident rate and the aircraft's reputation for being a "widow maker."

Training bombs are prepared for loading aboard an AT-11 training flight. The AT-11 carried ten 100-pound M38A2 practice bombs or ten 100-pound, general-purpose, high-explosive bombs. A training flight would have two student bombardiers; one would drop, while the other would film the bomb run for scoring.

A tower on the New Mexico Proving Grounds holds a wireframe aircraft target for variable timing fuse testing. The proving grounds comprised over 30,000 acres south of the airport to the Manzano foothills. The variable timing fuse, otherwise known as the proximity fuse, was a critical technology used to stop the Nazi's V-1 "buzz bomb" attacks on Britain. Development of the fuse was also known as "New Mexico's second best secret" during World War II, after the Manhattan Project.

A bomb strikes during a competition out on the range. Numerous bomb ranges were located on desert lands north, west, and south of Albuquerque, where targets in the shape of ships and bullseyes were laid out. Unexploded ordnance and concrete "bombs" have been found at the sites into the 21st century, though significant remediation has taken place.

Bombardier trainees celebrate winning the AAF Flying Training Command's Bombing Olympics, receiving the prestigious Pickle Barrel award. The creator of the highly accurate Norden bombsight, Carl Norden, was credited with the apocryphal statement that bombardiers "could hit a pickle barrel from 20,000 feet," with the device.

Kirtland AAF maintainers work on the tail section of an AT-11. Aircraft maintainers are the unsung heroes of the flying world, working wonders on their winged machines. While the Air Depot Training Station graduated maintainers to assist the war effort around the world, Kirtland Field required its own cadre to help repair aircraft damaged by students and the professional pilots.

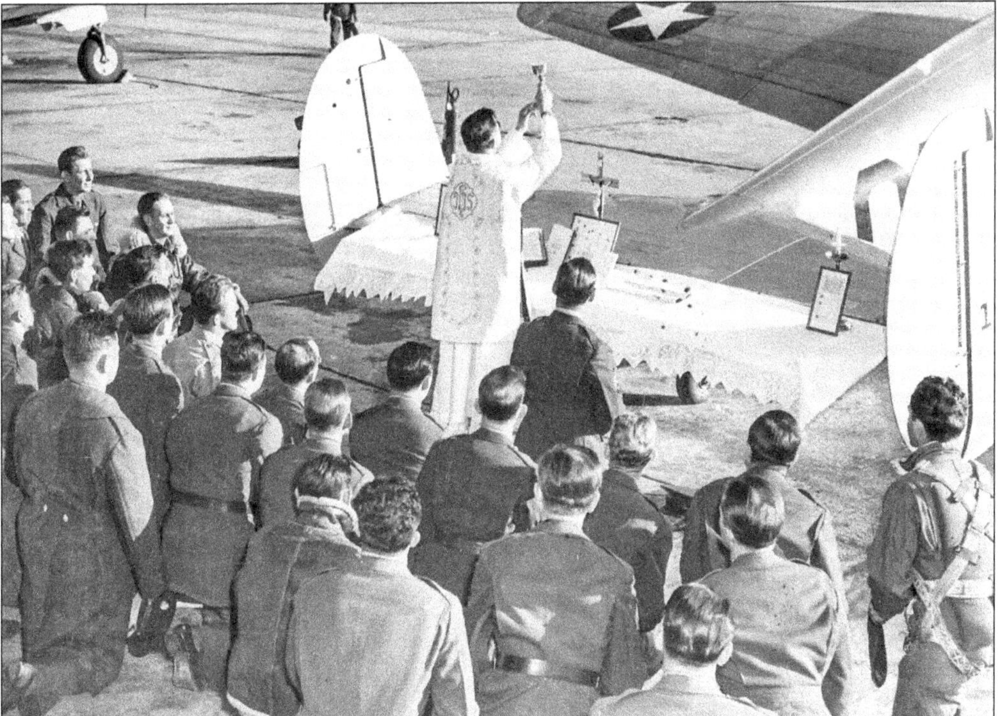

Kirtland's Catholic chaplain performs Christmas Mass services on the tail of an AT-11.

This aerial view of Sandia Base in 1946 shows rows of war-weary aircraft awaiting disposal. The planes sit at the edge of the old Oxnard Field, and the original airport buildings can be seen near center. Many of these buildings would become the nucleus of the AFSWP's Sandia Base and Sandia National Laboratories.

Hundreds of bombers await destruction at Sandia Base in 1946. After the war, the ample acreage around Sandia Base held hundreds of war aircraft awaiting demilitarization, melting down, and disposal.

Antiaircraft guns sit at the New Mexico Proving Grounds awaiting their next aerial targets for proximity fuse testing. Eight million proximity fuses were produced by the end of World War II.

Air Force Day—September 18, 1948—showed Albuquerque citizens some of the aircraft and equipment in use by the US military. In the background is a C-97 Stratofreighter, a cargo variant of the B-29 bomber. In the foreground, children climb on a V-2 rocket from White Sands Proving Grounds near Las Cruces.

A B-36 is on display during the August 1949 Kirtland Open House. Kirtland, as the hub of weapon modification efforts and atomic storage, saw many days of "aluminum overcast."

A B-50 sits atop the atomic bomb load pit. Kirtland AAF served as an aerial transfer point for men and materiel going to Los Alamos for the Manhattan Project. A special pit for loading atomic weapons was built in a remote location near the runway. On July 27, 1945, three Silverplate B-29s (42-65386, 44-86346, 44-86347) departed Kirtland with parts for three Fat Man bombs, bound for Tinian.

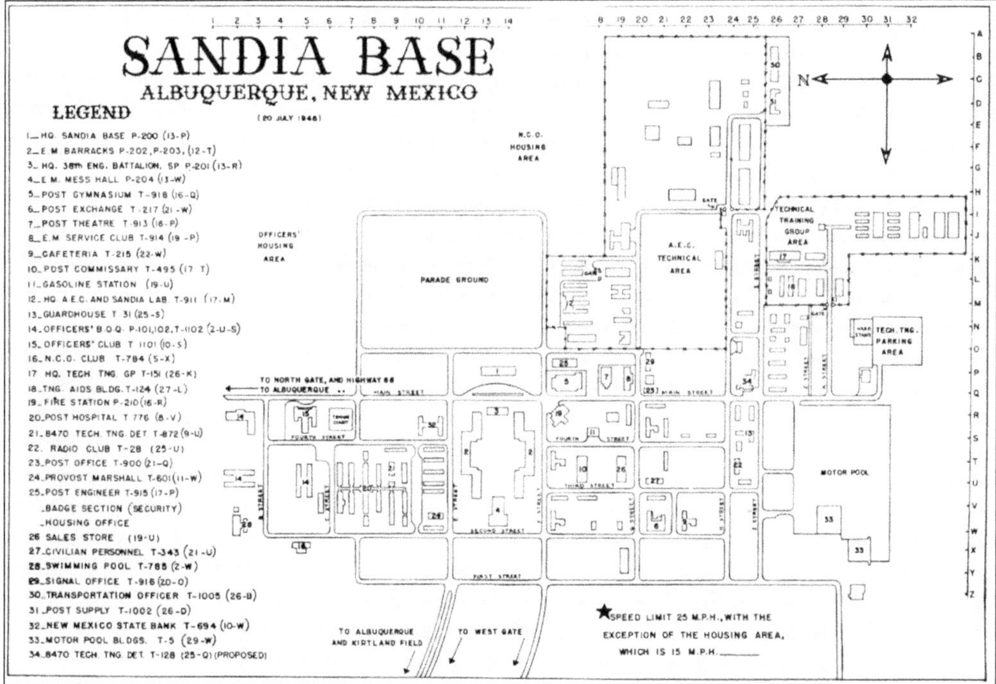

This map of Sandia Base from July 1948 shows many of the areas familiar to people working at Kirtland today. The parade ground is now Hardin Field, the AEC technical area is part of Sandia National Laboratories, and the Technical Training Group Area contains portions of the Defense Nuclear Weapons School. (Courtesy of Defense Nuclear Weapons School.)

Three unidentified members of a 4925th Test Group (Atomic) B-36 crew pose in front of their aircraft in 1955. During Operation Teapot in 1955, the B-36 was used for airdrop on three separate shots—HA (high altitude), WASP, and WASP Prime. The WASP Prime blast occurred roughly five hours after APPLE-1, marking the first time that two nuclear explosions were set off in one day.

The USAF's first operational jet bomber, a B-45 Tornado, taxis at Kirtland. The B-45 was an early part of the nation's nuclear deterrent but was soon superseded in the late 1950s by the B-47 Stratojet and B-58 Hustler, both of which could fly faster.

Lt. Gen. Curtis LeMay (center) visits Kirtland in 1948. Best known for being the commander of Strategic Air Command (1948–1957), LeMay was a strong proponent for strategic bombardment. His experience as the 305th Bomb Group commander in Europe and the firebombing of Tokyo helped solidify his belief that "the bomber will always get through." LeMay helped propel the nuclear delivery mission of SAC into the public's eye, both allied and adversary.

Alert hangars for F-86 air defense fighters reside immediately off the main runway. Air defense of New Mexico was vitally important due to the presence of Los Alamos, Sandia Base, Manzano Base, and the testing facilities at White Sands.

The 4925th Test Group (Atomic) shield shows a circular cloud with aviation wings above and a nuclear symbol below, signifying the unit's mission of nuclear delivery through aeronautical means. The unit was established in 1948 as the 3170th Special Weapons Group, but it was redesignated the 4925th in 1949. The unit was inactivated on August 31, 1961, having been at Kirtland the entire length of its existence.

A 4950th Test Group (Nuclear) crew dressed in operational flight gear stands in front of a B-47 (left). In the background, other aircraft belonging to the 4950th—a B-36 (center) and B-50 (right)—represent the diverse fleet owned by the AFSWC's "Atomic Air Force." Such a diverse fleet—propeller driven to jet engines—enabled war planners to get the most accurate picture of weapon effects possible at the time.

From left to right, Capt. Howard E. Luber, Airman 3rd Class Walter Levine, Edward Beer, and Maj. Robert E. Osborn try new test uniform combinations in the summer of 1954. While not adopted force-wide, the pith helmet and shorts were popular in the Pacific during the atmospheric nuclear tests of the 1950s and 1960s.

Construction starts on a new taxiway and parking apron. In the background, petroleum, oil, and lubricants (POL) storage and Wherry housing can be seen. The POL storage area would cause problems decades later after fuel leaks in the Albuquerque aquifer were discovered.

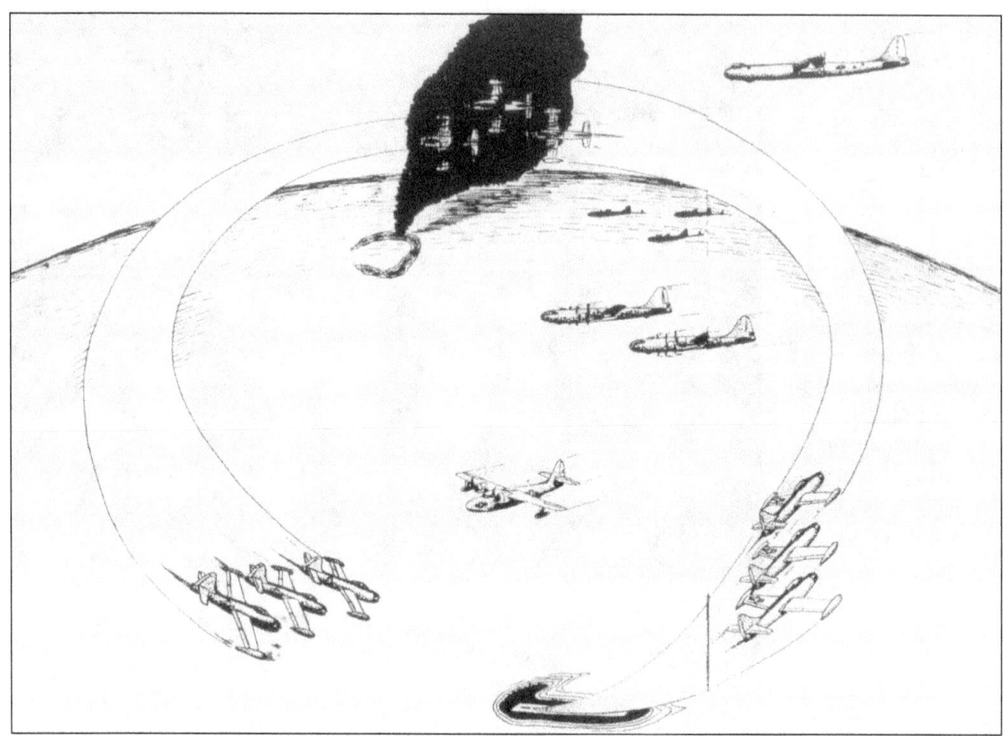

The profile for an atomic sampling mission shows the simplicity of the flight path. At a predetermined time after detonation and growth of the "mushroom" cloud, a specially modified B-57 Canberra flies through the cloud. Special inlets on the aircraft allow for collection of radioactive particles present in the air. Designers use the data to determine efficiencies in the weapon—if all of the material was consumed, for example.

A B-57 flies in view of a nuclear blast during Operation Hardtack in 1958. At the conclusion of the Hardtack series, the United States announced a testing moratorium. The subsequent belief that nuclear testing ceased permanently helped US authorities decide to downsize the 4950th Test Group and its operational squadrons.

Three

WINDS OF CHANGE, 1960–1979

From a national security perspective, the 1960s brought massive change across the military services. The start of the decade saw the Air Force Special Weapons Center reorganize from the voluntary test moratorium. During the moratorium, the 4925th Test Group (Atomic), 4950th Test Group (Nuclear), and 4935th Air Base Group were inactivated. The only nuclear-related squadron to remain at Kirtland after 1961 was the 4926th Test Squadron (Sampling). Redesignated as the 1211th Test Squadron (Sampling), the unit continued to support the final atmospheric tests until 1963. Recognizing the continuing need for atmospheric sampling, the 57th Weather Reconnaissance Squadron's W/RB-57F Canberras took the mantle from 1964 until 1974.

After the Limited Test Ban Treaty was signed in 1963, the Air Force Weapons Laboratory was created to simulate nuclear effects such as transient radiation, X-rays, and electromagnetic pulse (EMP) to determine vulnerabilities on US weapon systems. Later in the decade, AFWL would gain the directed energy (laser and high-power microwave) mission.

During the Cuban Missile Crisis in 1962, New Mexico Air National Guard pilots from the 150th Tactical Fighter Group were activated for federal service. The rest of the 1960s saw the 150th activated again for the Pueblo Crisis and the Vietnam War. F-100 Super Sabre pilots and maintainers deployed to Tuy Hoa Air Base, Republic of Vietnam, from May 1968 through May 1969. The air war over Vietnam saw 150th Tactical Fighter Group pilots accumulate over 6,000 sorties and numerous medals for valor and bravery.

As a cost-saving measure in the wake of the Vietnam War, the Nixon administration directed the merger of the three bases—Kirtland, Sandia, and Manzano. In 1971, the merger was complete, creating what we know today as Kirtland Air Force Base.

In 1976, the Air Force moved Military Airlift Command's Aerospace Rescue and Recovery Service training to Kirtland. This move jumpstarted the base's flying mission after a downturn following the AFSWC's inactivation. The 1550 Aircrew Training and Test Wing helicopter and fixed-wing aircrews arrived at Kirtland on February 20, 1976, bringing the pararescue mission to Albuquerque.

An AFSWC aircraft flies over parts of Northwest New Mexico during the winter of 1960 (above). Winter storms through the Navajo Nation prevented supplies and livestock feed from being delivered. Air drops (below) were used to expeditiously move needed supplies, such as these bags of potatoes, until the snow thaw.

A B-57 Canberra is scrubbed during decontamination at Indian Springs AFB after a nuclear test. The Kirtland-based 4926th Test Squadron (Sampling), and later, the 1211th Test Squadron, used the high-altitude-capable B-57 during atmospheric tests until 1962. Later missions monitored underground tests for escaping radioactivity, and monitoring of other nations' nuclear tests.

An AFSWC gate guard waves traffic onto Kirtland. Air Force Systems Command was formed from Air Research and Development Command in 1961. AFSC ran materiel procurement for the Air Force, while its subordinate unit AFSWC concentrated on nuclear systems. AFSC transferred the base to Military Airlift Command responsibility in 1977.

The "Beetle" was a 50-ton nuclear equipment handling vehicle built by General Electric for repairs on aircraft nuclear propulsion systems. AFSWC transported the vehicle to the Nevada Test Site after cancellation of the nuclear aircraft project. The vehicle's cab was surrounded by one-foot-thick lead walls and contained a periscope, public address system, air conditioning, and (of course) radiation detectors.

Col. Raymond Gilbert (1919–2013) unveils the sign to the Air Force Weapons Laboratory in 1963. Gilbert served as the first director and commander of AFWL until 1966. Work for AFWL's nuclear effects mission was increasing throughout the 1960s, since the cessation of atmospheric nuclear testing after the Limited Nuclear Test Ban Treaty was signed on August 5, 1963.

The first four females to attend Non-Commissioned Officers (NCO) Academy are seen at Kirtland. The men-only policy changed in July 1969, and Air Force Systems Command held the first integrated course. The first four Women of the Air Force to attend were, from left to right, S.Sgt. Earline Taylor, S.Sgt. Catherine Jones, S.Sgt. Cecil Lofton, and T.Sgt. Yo Vonne L. Menzel.

This c. 1970 aerial view of the Nuclear Weapons School facilities shows the original Quonset huts still in use behind the main buildings. Thousands of nuclear weapons technicians, planners, and responders attended the campus, which extended along the southern end of Wyoming Boulevard. (Courtesy of Defense Nuclear Weapons School.)

The Kirtland NCO Club burned to the ground on January 6, 1968. After the fire, the club moved into the old Officer's Club building.

An F-100 from the 150th Tactical Fighter Group approaches Tuy Hoa Air Base, Republic of Vietnam. The 150th TFG personnel returned to Albuquerque in June 1969 after amassing an impressive combat record: 6,000 sorties flown, with one pilot killed in action and two listed as missing in action.

Pictured is a 150th Tactical Fighter Group A-7D in the mid-1970s. The deployment of the A-7D to the Air National Guard was unique, since the aircraft was still in use with active duty wings at the time. Prior to this, Air National Guard units flew aircraft that were older than their active duty counterparts.

Miss Kirtland Pat Abeyta presents coins commemorating 40 years of commercial aviation in Albuquerque to a Thunderbirds member on November 16, 1969. The Thunderbirds flew their brand-new F-4E Phantom IIs during their air show at kirtland, having switched from F-100s the previous year.

The garrison of Manzano Base is shown in this undated photograph. Financial concerns from the Vietnam War forced the Nixon administration to merge the three bases in 1971. Today, the site contains a Department of Energy training center.

The front of the National Atomic Museum displays two Navy Terrier surface-to-air missiles (above). The museum originally began as the Sandia Atomic Museum in 1969 but was renamed the National Atomic Museum in 1973. The name change reflected the growing audience and recognition as the only public museum in the world that preserved the history of nuclear weapons. The open bay (left) displays many unclassified weapons engineering models. One of the more interesting displays at the museum showed two weapon casings from a 1966 aircraft accident over Palomares, Spain. (Courtesy of the National Museum of Nuclear Science and History.)

The heraldic imagery for the 1550th Aircrew Training and Test Wing clearly shows its primary equipment via a rotor blade atop a sword. The 1550th ATTW was activated at Hill Air Force Base, Utah, in 1973, but moved to Kirtland in 1976. After the end of the Cold War, four-digit units were abolished, and the 1550th was redesignated the 542nd Crew Training Wing, assuming host responsibility for Kirtland from 1991 to 1994.

The c. 1986 emblem of the 1551st Flying Training Squadron includes typical warrior motifs, such as the sword. What is unique to the logo however, is the inclusion of the Zia symbol in the background, along with mountains and desert, signifying the unit's home in New Mexico. After its inactivation in 2007, the now 551st Special Operations Squadron resides at Cannon Air Force Base, near Clovis. (Courtesy of Air Force Historical Research Agency.)

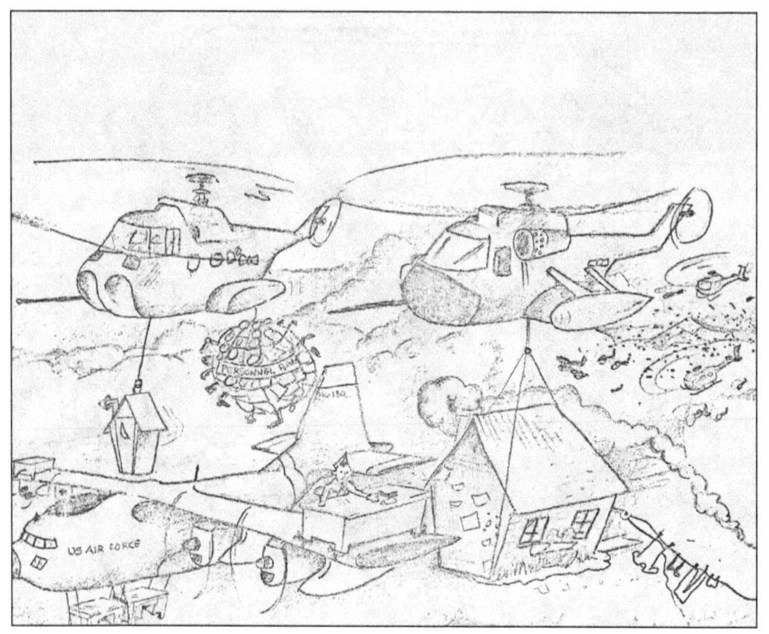

In this drawing, the 1550th ATTW's move from Hill Air Force Base, Utah, to Albuquerque in 1976 is humorously illustrated. The stylized HH-3 Jolly Green helicopters are lifting a house (complete with clothesline), a personnel bag (presumably filled with personnel), and an outhouse. HC-130s were used, too, picking up a deskbound worker and extra office furniture.

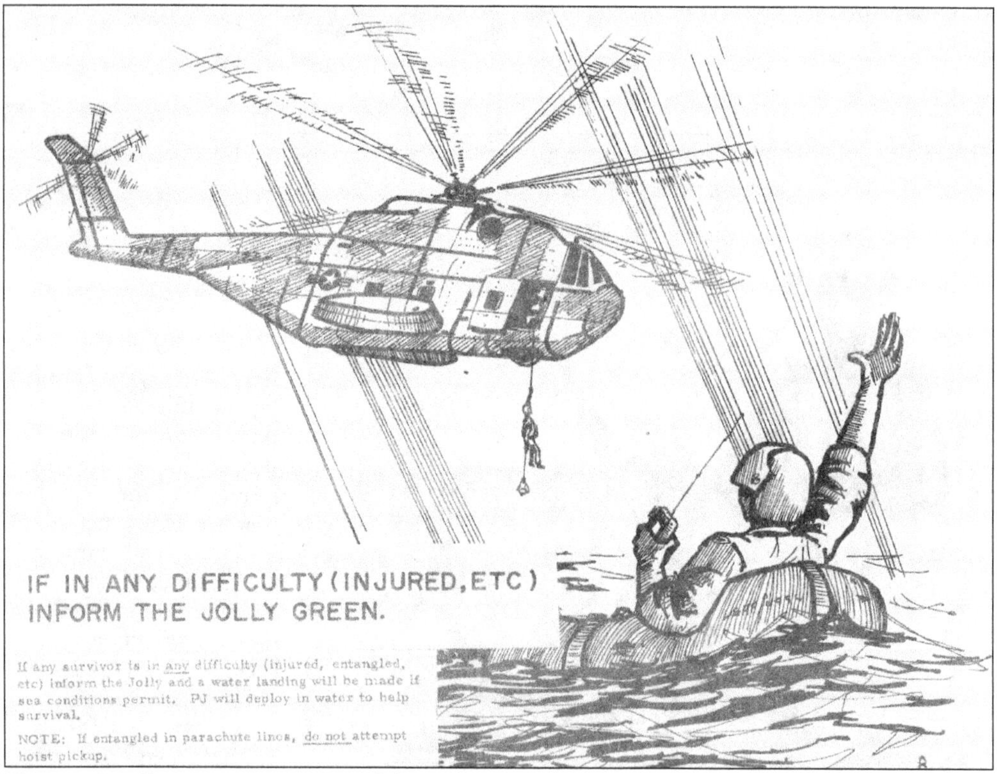

IF IN ANY DIFFICULTY (INJURED, ETC)
INFORM THE JOLLY GREEN.

If any survivor is in any difficulty (injured, entangled, etc) inform the Jolly and a water landing will be made if sea conditions permit. PJ will deploy in water to help survival.

NOTE: If entangled in parachute lines, do not attempt hoist pickup.

This graphic illustrates one mission of the HH-3: water-borne rescue. If a survivor was incapacitated, the helicopter could land in the water to assist with pickup. Folksinger James P. Durham's song "Jolly Green" describes a pilot's emotions after being shot down and awaiting rescue: "Sounds of rotors now I've heard / Here comes that great big whirly bird / The PJ's cable now I've seen on Jolly Green / My Jolly Green."

Airman 1st Class Barbara Orr, Miss Bicentennial Kirtland, welcomed Albuquerque residents to the base open house on June 19, 1976. Orr was a graphics specialist with the 1550th ATTW.

Airman Annette Hastings (center) briefs Valley High School Air Force Junior ROTC cadet Bernadette Leal on the operation of a UH-1 Huey helicopter. The senior year cadets spent part of a day touring the 1550th ATTW.

This is a c. 1972 aerial shot of Kirtland, the Albuquerque International Sunport, and Southeast Albuquerque. The dense clusters of buildings at far right are housing for base personnel and their families.

An H-3 floats at Elephant Butte reservoir during a training exercise. The H-3 served for decades in the Aerospace Rescue and Recover Service (later renamed Air Rescue Service), with the HH-3E known as the Jolly Green Giant.

M.Sgt. Wayne Fisk stores his parachute during pararescue training at Kirtland in 1979. Fisk was involved in the Son Tay POW camp raid in November 1970, and the SS *Mayaguez* in 1975. He was honored as one of the US Jaycees 10 Outstanding Young Men in America, the first USAF enlisted man to be honored. Fisk later led the effort to establish the Air Force Enlisted Heritage Hall at Maxwell Air Force Base, Alabama.

The Air Force Contract Management Division (AFCMD) moved to Kirtland in October 1972. When the Air Force Special Weapons Center inactivated in April 1976, AFCMD assumed host responsibilities through the 4900th Air Base Wing. Aside from running Kirtland from 1976 to 1977, the AFCMD had the responsibility of managing Air Force plant representative offices, test site offices, and contract support detachments across the world.

A Cray-1 supercomputer sits at AFWL's Air Force Supercomputer Center at Kirtland. Developed in the mid-1970s by Cray Research, these supercomputers were defined by their speed (160 million floating point operations per second), data-size (64-bit), and 8-megabyte main memory. In 1983, a Government Accounting Office report found that the lab's research did not justify the continued lease and operation of these expensive computer systems.

The Air Force Test and Evaluation Center was established in 1974 at Kirtland, designed as a small agency that would borrow most of the equipment, personnel, and facilities needed for field testing. In 1983, with an expanded mission, it was renamed Air Force Operational Test and Evaluation Center. Today, it is responsible for testing every major Air Force weapon system.

The headquarters building of the 1606th Air Base Wing was originally constructed as an expansion of the DASA Nuclear Weapons School in 1966. After the inactivation of the AFSWC, and the Contract Management Division's control of the base, Military Airlift Command assumed responsibility for Kirtland and activated the 1606th as the host unit. This building currently serves as headquarters of the 377th Air Base Wing.

This is an early artist's conception of the Trestle. Note that the concept included two separate wooden platforms, each with a separate wire net, for simultaneous testing of multiple weapon systems. Other simulators, such as ACHILLES, ARES, and ATHAMAS, were also used at Kirtland to test various EMP effects on aircraft electronic systems.

Construction on the Trestle Electromagnetic Pulse Simulator started in 1978. Officially known as ATLAS I (AFWL Transmission-Line Aircraft Simulator), the location is a large-volume, bounded-wave EMP simulator used to expose aircraft and equipment to simulated effects of high-altitude EMP, from an electric field of over 10 million volts. The facility was the brainchild of Dr. Carl Baum, an electromagnetics engineer from AFWL.

This view of the Trestle under construction shows the Central Ground Plane Wedge, a steel wave-focusing structure, surrounded by snow. The wedge was 250 feet long and 240 feet high and was believed to be the tallest structure in Albuquerque at the time of construction.

This view of the side of the Trestle shows the enormous amount of lumber used for its construction. For EMP testing, metal connectors and fasteners cause unwanted reflections in the environment. The solution was resin-impregnated all-wood bolts. Using an estimated 6.5 million board feet of glue-laminated timber, the Trestle is believed to be the largest all-wood structure in the world.

An E-4B Advanced Airborne Command Post sits near the Trestle during testing in 1979. The mission of the E-4B, known as the "Doomsday Plane," necessitated testing for survival in a post-nuclear environment. (Courtesy of the National Archives)

Four

Strategic Modernization, 1980–1999

The election of Ronald Reagan in 1980 saw many changes under his Strategic Modernization Program. Kirtland landmarks, such as the Air Force Weapons Laboratory's TRESTLE, were used to ensure the viability of US weapon systems in a nuclear environment

Military actions in the late 1980s and early 1990s, such as the invasion of Panama and Operation Desert Storm, saw Kirtland-trained pararescue aircrews go into combat. Additionally, the 150th Tactical Fighter Group deployed security police members to Saudi Arabia.

After the end of the Cold War, changes to organization structures on Kirtland occurred in earnest. The 1550th ATTW was redesignated the 542nd Crew Training Wing in 1994, only to be replaced by the 58th Special Operations Wing. The 58th remained the premier training site for Air Force special operations and combat search and rescue aircrews.

Additionally, the wing responds to worldwide contingencies and provides search and rescue support to the region. Aircrews from Kirtland AFB have participated in more than 300 rescue operations to date, and its members have been credited with saving more than 225 lives.

A B-52G is pulled along the ramp to the test stand. An AFWL study in 1970 used the B-52G as the basis for design parameters of the Trestle, such as turning radius, load weights, and overall test stand dimensions. The B-52G test took place in fiscal year 1981, one year after initial operating capability was declared.

A C-5A Galaxy takes off from Kirtland's runway, with the Manzano Mountains in the background.

Dr. Don Alberts (1935–2010) earned his doctorate in history at the University of New Mexico in 1975. He was the chief historian at Kirtland from 1977 to 1988 and wrote the seminal history of the base in 1985 with Allan Putnam. Alberts's interests in history also covered early aviation in Albuquerque and the Civil War in New Mexico.

Two eras of pararescuemen stand in formation outside Chapman Hall on West Kirtland. Chapman Hall was named for Capt. Peter H. Chapman II, who was killed during a rescue attempt in the Quang Tri province of Vietnam on April 6, 1972. The building was dedicated in his name on May 6, 1977.

In this late 1980s photograph, Staff Sergeant Wilkinson receives an Air Force Achievement Medal.

Col. Charles R. Holland, commander of the 1550th ATTW, greets Santa during Christmas festivities. Holland was the vice commander and later commander of the 1550th from June 1988 through June 1991. He finished his career as commander of US Special Operations Command in 2003.

Volunteers show off the improvements to the Rescue Museum. From 1976 to 1990, Chapman Hall served as the home of a museum, before expansion of the building's classroom space forced the wing to close it down. Most of these artifacts eventually came under the administration of the pararescue schoolhouse at Kirtland Air Force Base, where they are currently displayed.

Kirtland's jail held bunks and lockers for incarcerated service members. In March 1950, a fire at the Sandia Base guardhouse killed 14 military prisoners.

An interior shot of the security police office shows the officer on duty sporting her service pistol while working administrative duties. On military installations, civilian law enforcement has limited jurisdiction, so law breakers must be dealt with by military law enforcement.

Col. Roland Page, commander of the 1550th ATTW, exits during his "fini flight," a commander's ceremonial last flight in the unit's aircraft, in the summer of 1989.

1550th ATTW helicopter maintainers pose in front of the HH-3. In 1982, an overseas rescue unit requested an HH-3 from Kirtland. The helicopter was taken apart, shipped via C-5 Galaxy, and reassembled in less than a week.

In this c. 1995 photograph, the Wyoming gate is the primary entrance for Kirtland Air Force Base. When Sandia Base opened in 1946 complete with guard towers and fences, Wyoming Gate was called "Main Street" on base, as there was nothing in the vicinity off base.

Three aircraft familiar to Kirtland's pararescue personnel—from top to bottom, MH-53, HH-3, and UH-1—fly in formation over Albuquerque.

The squadron bar inside the Aerospace Ground Equipment facility (pictured around the late 1980s), harkens back to an earlier era of US Air Force history.

The Consolidated Base Personnel Office on Kirtland sports a fallout shelter sign to the right of its main entrance.

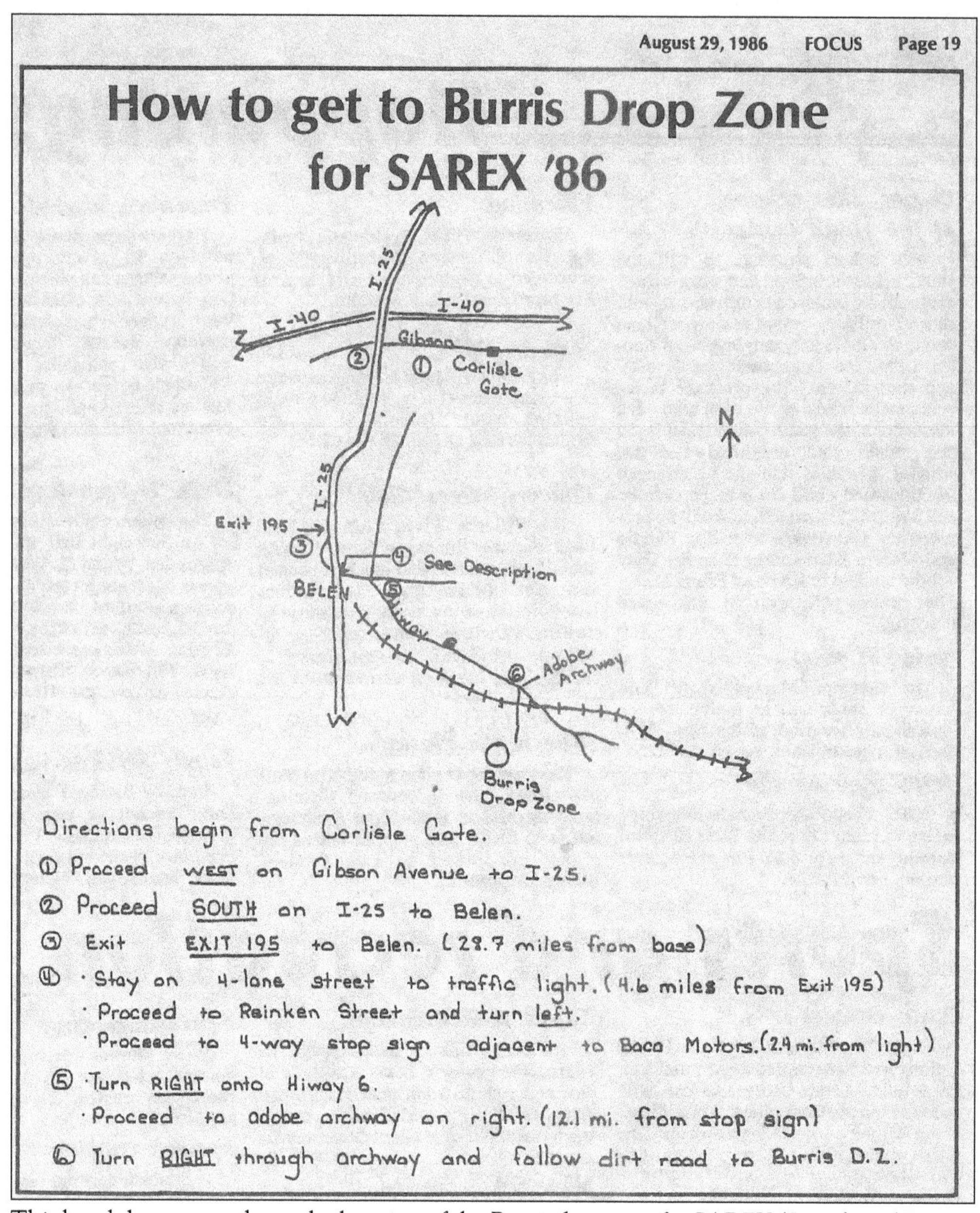

August 29, 1986 FOCUS Page 19

How to get to Burris Drop Zone for SAREX '86

Directions begin from Carlisle Gate.

① Proceed WEST on Gibson Avenue to I-25.

② Proceed SOUTH on I-25 to Belen.

③ Exit EXIT 195 to Belen. (28.7 miles from base)

④ · Stay on 4-lane street to traffic light. (4.6 miles from Exit 195)
· Proceed to Reinken Street and turn left.
· Proceed to 4-way stop sign adjacent to Baca Motors. (2.4 mi. from light)

⑤ · Turn RIGHT onto Hiway 6.
· Proceed to adobe archway on right. (12.1 mi. from stop sign)

⑥ Turn RIGHT through archway and follow dirt road to Burris D.Z.

This hand-drawn map shows the location of the Burris drop zone for SAREX (Search and Rescue Exercise) 86. Special Operations aircrews often use drop zones or airports in the nearby community to practice landing in various conditions.

The NKC-135 Airborne Laser Laboratory (ALL), s/n 55-3123, is pictured in flight. The experimental ALL program ran from 1975 to 1984 under the auspices of the Air Force Weapons Laboratory, and used a carbon-dioxide laser to intercept small air-to-air missiles and drones. The aircraft was retired and sent to the National Museum of the United States Air Force in Dayton, Ohio, in 1984.

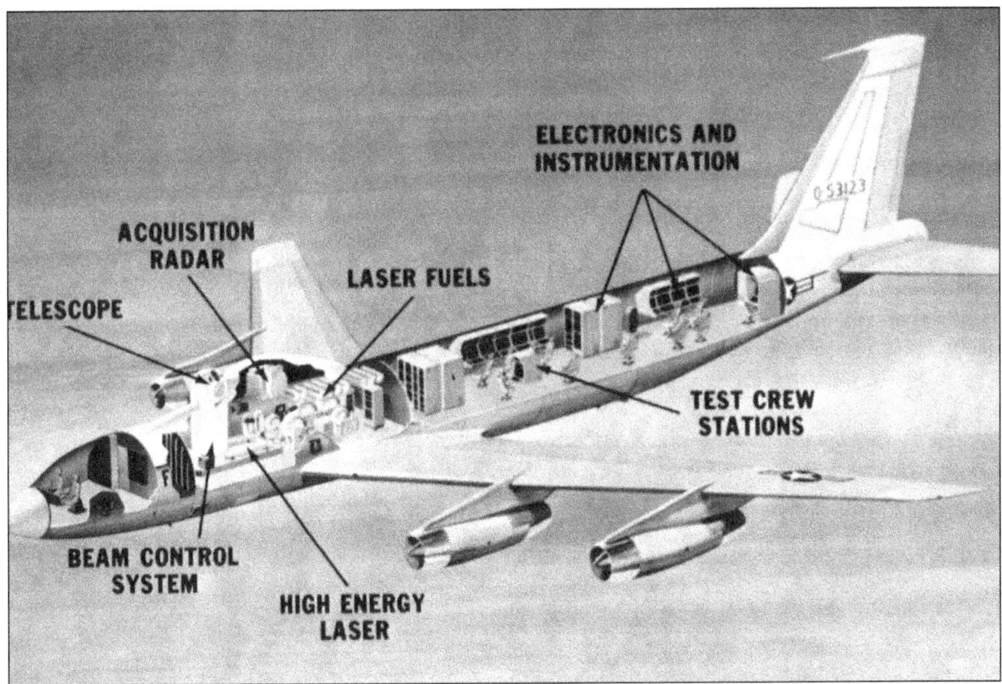

This illustrated cutaway of the NKC-135 shows the major interior compartments and equipment aboard the NKC-135 ALL aircraft. Interest in antimissile technologies surged after Operation Desert Storm's infamous SCUD missile attacks, and lessons learned from the ALL program transitioned into the YAL-1 Airborne Laser program.

This aerial view of the AFWL complex in the 1980s also shows the hangars of the 1550th ATTW and its contingent of rescue helicopters. By the early 1990s, AFWL would combine with Phillips Lab and many other organizations around the country to become the Air Force Research Laboratory. The tree-lined street is Carlisle Boulevard.

A new Kirtland base commissary opened in 1989. Each uniformed service controlled its own commissary grocery stores until the creation of the Defense Commissary Agency in 1990.

The opening of the Kirtland Base Exchange (BX) is pictured in the late 1980s. As popular destinations for base personnel, base exchanges usually contain a retail store, food court, and various shops mirroring an indoor shopping mall. A replacement BX was opened on June 28, 2013, right next to the "old" facility.

Inter-service Nuclear Weapons School students wear radiological contamination protective gear during a Nuclear Emergency Team Operations class field exercise in April 1984. (Courtesy of National Archives.)

An MH-53 drops off a Navy SEAL team during training in New Mexico. The MH-53 Pave Low was initially designed to replace the HH-3 Jolly Green Giant search-and-rescue helicopter. Since downed aircrew extraction often took place at night, the HH-53 was refitted with low-light imagers, terrain-following radars, and radar warning receivers for self-protection.

An F-16 is tested at Phillips Laboratory anechoic chamber facilities in the 1990s. Note the "PL" (Philips Laboratory) tail code.

Pararescue personnel stand inside a C-130, preparing for a jump. Insertion of special operations personnel can take many paths, but the parachute jump is one of the quickest.

This c. 1990s view from the ground shows jumpers exiting a C-130 during a training exercise.

This is a representative example of an enlisted dormitory room in the 1990s. Unit commanders and first sergeants routinely conduct room inspections to ensure basic sanitary conditions are present in the dorms. This dorm contains a common feature of enlisted dorms of the era—a large stereo system.

This is an aerial view of Hardin Field in the 1980s. Note the lack of trees surrounding the field's perimeter. Sandia National Laboratory buildings are at top, and Wyoming Boulevard is at lower right.

Chief of staff of the Air Force Gen. Ronald Fogleman sits in the front seat of a 150th Fighter Wing F-16, with Capt. Thomas M. "Wheels" Wheeler in the rear seat during a flight in July 1995.

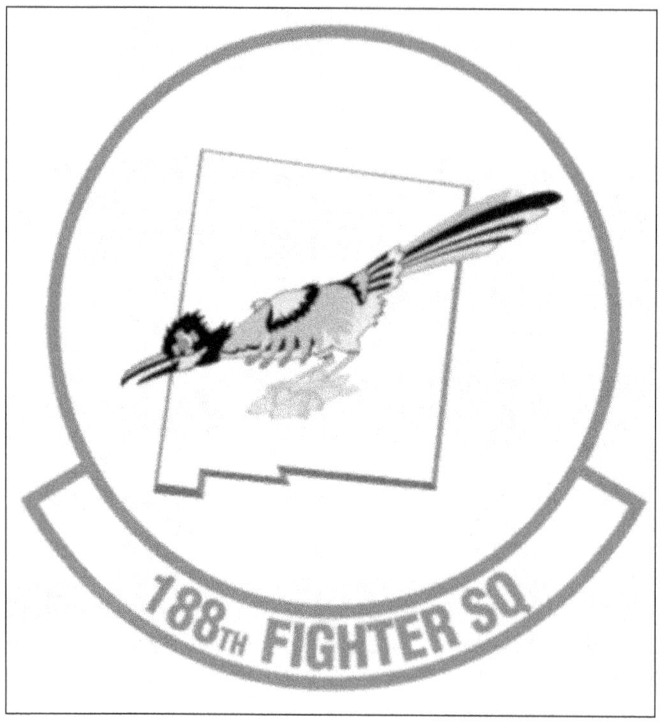

The 188th Fighter Squadron was assigned to the New Mexico Air National Guard in 1946 and federally recognized in 1947. The 188th is the primary operations unit of the 150th wing. The unit was redesignated the 188th Rescue Wing in January 2013, flying HC-130s, CV-22s, and HH-60G Pave Hawks.

The Air Force Office of Security Police headquarters moved to Kirtland in 1978. In 1991, the organization was renamed Air Force Security Police Agency (AFSPA). AFSPA reported directly to the Air Force chief of security police. AFSPA was comprised of four directorates: security, law enforcement and training, resources, and corrections. After the Khobar Towers bombing in 1996, AFSPA moved to Lackland Air Force Base, Texas, in November 1997.

Due to geopolitical changes, the Defense Nuclear Agency was renamed the Defense Special Weapons Agency (DSWA) in 1996. While DSWA still had a charter to provide a center for nuclear technical expertise in the Defense Department, more attention was given to the Cooperative Threat Reduction Programs helping with nonproliferation of weapons technology around the world. Expansion of these responsibilities saw the organization renamed in 1998 to the Defense Threat Reduction Agency.

The Phillips Laboratory was dedicated in 1990. Gen. Samuel C. Phillips (1921–1990) was director of the Minuteman ICBM program, director of the Apollo Manned Lunar Landing Program, director of the National Security Agency (1972), and commander of Air Force Systems Command (1973). Phillips Lab was absorbed into the Air Force Research Laboratory (AFRL) in 1997, after consolidation of four laboratory facilities and the Air Force Office of Scientific Research. Here, Phillips's widow, Betty Ann Phillips, unveils the lab's logo.

Shiva Star is a high-powered pulse-powered test device developed by AFWL to test nuclear survivability in defense systems. The six banks of capacitors were able to hold 9.4 megajoules of energy before simultaneously releasing it toward the center area. On many occasions, "successful" tests created shrapnel caught by the surrounding equipment.

Five

Global War on Terror, 2000–Present

Soon after the devastating terror attacks of September 11, 2001, the Bush administration declared a worldwide "war on terror," involving open and covert military operations. Many members of the Kirtland Air Force Base community, military and civilian, deployed in support of the Global War on Terror throughout its many phases.

The start of the new millennium for Kirtland brought some of the previous century's old baggage with it. In 1999, Kirtland officials acknowledged a fuel spill that had been ongoing since 1953, when modernized fuel storage facilities were constructed. In 2015, the Air Force and New Mexico Environmental Department began a remediation plan to keep the underground fuel plume, last estimated at 24 million gallons, from contaminating several drinking water wells in northeast Albuquerque.

Since 2001, the wing has deployed more than 200 personnel in support of the Global War on Terror. On November 23, 2003, the 58th Special Operations Wing suffered its first casualty of the war when Maj. Steven Plumhoff, an MH-53J pilot, died in a helicopter crash while deployed to Afghanistan for Operation Enduring Freedom.

Pararescue trainees at Kirtland practice short-range target engagement with nine-millimeter pistols at the Department of Energy's range complex in Coyote Canyon. Pararescuemen, or "PJs" are routinely dispatched into dangerous situations for the recovery of downed aircrew members. By the end of their weapons training, students can squeeze off two headshots within seconds. (Courtesy of the National Archives.)

Two HH-60 Blackhawks fly over a meadow in the Jemez Mountains northwest of Albuquerque. The HH-60 replaced the Vietnam-era HH-3 Jolly Green for many mission profiles, working alongside the MH-53 Super Jolly Green Giant for rescue, recovery, and other special operations missions.

The 550th Special Operations Squadron, nicknamed "The Wolfpack," was one of the original squadrons to arrive at Kirtland in 1976 (as the 1550th Flying Training Squadron).

MC-130P Combat Shadow and MC-130H Combat Talon II aircraft taxi for takeoff during a readiness exercise in 2002. These variants supported special operations missions, such as infiltration, exfiltration, resupply, and air refueling (MC-130P) of special-ops helicopter and tilt-rotor aircraft.

The Air Force's first operational CV-22 Osprey tilt-rotor aircraft arrives at Kirtland on March 20, 2006. The aircraft was assigned to the 58th Special Operations Wing to train future Osprey pilots.

A 71st Special Operations Squadron CV-22 Osprey is refueled by a 522nd Special Operations Squadron MC-130J Combat Shadow II over New Mexico. After decades of supporting flight training in the HH-3E, HH-53, UH-1, and HH-43 helicopters and the HC-130P, HC-130N, and MC-130H/P, the squadron was inactivated in 2016.

MH-53J, s/n 66-14433 was the prototype for the Pave Low III program. The Pave Low concept first emerged during the Vietnam War, in response to a need for implementing a helicopter rescue platform capable of performing nighttime missions. It also became the first MH-53 to reach 10,000 flying hours. From 1991 to 2005, it participated in nine searches and four credited saves, and helped train more than 750 aircrew members.

A 58th Special Operations Wing HH-60 Pave Hawk refuels during a training mission over New Mexico.

The 351st Battlefield Airman Training Squadron activated at Kirtland on June 2, 2016. The training pipeline for "fifth-generation warriors" was consolidated in 2016 to integrate air and ground operations on the joint battlefield. Graduates operate as a ground component to solve ground problems with airpower, often embedding with conventional and special operations forces.

A 351st Battlefield Airmen Training Squadron student performs a fireman's carry on a "wounded" soldier during a mass casualty exercise on January 6, 2018. The exercise features a series of full mission profiles—skills required during combat and rescue ops—for combat rescue officers and pararescuemen.

A 351st Battlefield Airmen Training Squadron member treats a simulated injured soldier. 351st students managed to triage, treat, and transport all wounded while under simulated fire during a combat mass-casualty exercise.

Members of the 150th Fighter Wing perform maintenance on F-16 Fighting Falcon aircraft on February 5, 2005. Note the fin flash containing a Zia symbol, and the stylized representation of *Geococcyx californianus*, otherwise known as the (greater) roadrunner, on the tail. In 2010, the wing's F-16s were retired.

Brig. Gen. Andrew Salas (left) passes the 150th Special Operations Wing guidon to Col. Clark Highstrete (right), 150th Special Operations Wing commander, in 2013.

Members of the 210th Rapid Engineers Deployable Heavy Operations Repair Squadron Engineers (RED HORSE) stand at attention during a ceremony prior to their unit's first combat assignment. As one of the newest units to the New Mexico Air National Guard, the legacy of RED HORSE stretches to the Vietnam War, when the Air Force developed its own combat construction team like the US Navy construction battalions (Seabees).

US Air Force chief of staff Gen. David L. Goldfein (hand on chin) is briefed by a weapons system engineer at the Air Force Nuclear Weapon Center on October 19, 2017. The model of the upgraded B61-12 gravity bomb echoes a weapon design that was placed in service during 1963.

Chief Master Sergeant of the Air Force (CMSAF) Sam Parish (center) talks with chief master sergeants at the Kirtland NCO Academy in 2004. The auditorium was dedicated to Parish, who was the only former CMSAF to graduate as honor graduate in Kirtland's NCOA class 64-D. Until its closure in 2009, the Kirtland NCOA was the oldest continuously operated enlisted professional military education academy, originally opening in 1955.

A Caterpillar 980C Wheeled Excavator demolishes old housing units at Kirtland in August 2003. New privatized units were built, replacing Wherry and Capehart housing built in the 1950s. (Courtesy of the National Archives.)

Members of the Commemorative Air Force unload a World War II–era AT-11 Kansan at the Moriarty Airport in 2003. The AT-11 provided bombardier and navigation training at many airfields around New Mexico and was a mainstay in the skies above Albuquerque during World War II.

The Air Force Nuclear Weapons Center (AFNWC) was established on March 31, 2006, to synchronize all aspects of nuclear materiel management. The center has about 1,100 personnel and consists of four directorates: Air Delivered Capabilities; Intercontinental Ballistic Missile (ICBM) Systems; Nuclear Command, Control, and Communications Integration; and Nuclear Technology and Interagency. (Courtesy of the Air Force Historical Research Agency.)

AFNWC headquarters occupies a location on the former Sandia Base.

From left to right, AFNWC commander Maj. Gen. Scott Jansson inducts Donald Cook, AFNWC vice commander Col. George Farfour, and Eric Single; Eileen Ball and Katrina Benjamin representing their father Benjamin Benjamin; and inductees Jeffrey Bean and James "Al" Moyers into the Order of the Nucleus, honoring their work with nuclear weapons.

Brig. Gen. Sandra Finan (right) assumes command of the Air Force Nuclear Weapons Center in a ceremony on February 7, 2013. Gen. Janet Wolfenbarger, commander of Air Force Materiel Command (left) was the presiding officer.

Starting in Quonset huts and old Civilian Conservation Corps buildings on the edge of the old Oxnard Field, the Defense Nuclear Weapons School was established on January 1, 1947. These are the instructors from C Branch Technical Training Group photographed in October 1950. (Courtesy of Defense Nuclear Weapons School.)

Celebrating its 70th anniversary in 2017, past and present faculty, alumni, friends, and family attended an open house hosted in the Defense Nuclear Weapons School's unclassified hallway museum. (Courtesy of Defense Nuclear Weapons School.)

The DNWS delivers instructor-led courses to provide training for nuclear weapons core competencies and weapons of mass destruction accident response for Department of Defense, national laboratories personnel, and other agencies.

From left to right, Lt. Col. Christopher Picinni, Capt. Nate Larson, 20th Air Force commander Maj. Gen. Anthony Cotton, Capt. Kerry Dubuisson, and Capt. Greg Carter pose in front of an E-6B Mercury at Kirtland in 2016. The aircrew accompanied General Cotton on a nationwide tour aboard the Airborne National Command Post.

Members of the 377th Security Forces Squadron pose with their unit guidon during the Bataan Memorial Death March at White Sands Missile Range, New Mexico.

Chief M.Sgt. Thomas F. Good (right), 20th Air Force command chief, speaks with defenders from the 377th Weapons Systems Security Squadron at Kirtland on July 18, 2017.

The parents of Sr. Amn. Jason D. Cunningham receive his Air Force Cross posthumously during a ceremony at Kirtland on September 13, 2002. Cunningham was killed in action in Afghanistan during Operation Anaconda.

Airman Vanessa Dobos, pictured inside the door of an HH-60 Pave Hawk, stands next to her weapon, a 7.62-millimeter M134 Minigun machine gun. Dobos became the first female aerial gunner in the US Air Force after graduation from the technical school in 2002. During rescues, aerial gunners such as Dobos provide cover for PJs while retrieving downed aircrew members.

Richard Rast, AFRL senior engineer, manages the lab's small telescope project for the Satellite Assessment Center.

The Starfire Optical Range (SOR) 3.5-meter telescope is the second largest telescope in the Department of Defense. Dr. Robert Q. Fugate, seen at lower right, pioneered the use of adaptive optics at SOR that eliminate atmospheric distortion and provide sharper images for scientists.

This computer-generated drawing shows the XSS-10, part of AFRL's eXperimental Small Satellite Microsatellite Demonstration program. This new class of low-cost satellites—referred to as "micro-satellites"—weigh less than 200 pounds. AFRL's Space Vehicles Directorate at Kirtland serves as the Air Force's center of excellence for space technology research and development.

Rep. Heather A. Wilson shakes hands with Col. Kathleen D. Close, 377th Air Base Wing commander, on April 29, 2002, during her visit to Kirtland with Pres. George W. Bush. Wilson, a US Air Force Academy graduate, became secretary of the Air Force in 2017.

Chief M.Sgt. Juliet Gudgel (left), command chief master sergeant of Air Education and Training Command, is escorted by two 58th Special Operations Wing personnel on November 27, 2017, while a CV-22 Osprey sits in the background. The 58th's training mission fits uniquely between real-world operations with Air Force Special Operations Command and the training mission of AETC.

Tom Berardinelli, 377th Air Base Wing director of staff, briefs the public on the status of the jet fuel plume clean-up. The spill possibly began in the 1950s, based on analysis of the samples and ranges from 6 to 24 million gallons of fuel. As a comparison, the 1989 *Exxon Valdez* spill discharged 12 million gallons of oil into Prince William Sound.

Base commander Col. John Kubinec (right) conducts a tour for Albuquerque mayor Richard J. Berry at the base's bulk fuel facility site on January 23, 2013. During the tour, both men spoke about the fuel spill plume, stating, "The Air Force has taken ownership of this issue and has committed to the long term to make sure this is cleaned up."

This is a c. 2012 aerial view of Kirtland Air Force Base. The base covers 52,000 acres and has not changed in size since consolidation with Sandia Base and Manzano Base in 1971. However,

the missions supported have multiplied from the sleepy airfield that began training mechanics, bombardiers, and glider pilots seven decades earlier.

Today, Team Kirtland consists of agencies throughout the government—units from all four military services, total force representation from the Reserves and National Guard, and interagency partners from the Department of Energy, Homeland Security, and Sandia National Laboratories, just to name a few.

Six

Memorials

Kirtland contains several memorials—some markers, and others aircraft on display. Each display symbolizes men and women who sacrificed something of themselves for the security of the nation and the hope for freedom.

There is truth in the words "All gave some, and some gave all" at Kirtland Air Force Base. Notable memorials on base include the following:

Hardin Field, located on the east side of Kirtland near the Sandia National Laboratories campus. The field includes markers from Kirtland Field training classes.

Marquez Park, located across from the Base Exchange, Commissary. The park includes a memorial plaque, picnic tables with grills, and an expansive covered play park for children.

Rescue Memorial Park, on the west side of Kirtland, near the Pararescue Training School. Many rotary and fixed-wing aircraft are on display, representing search-and-rescue and special operations throughout the decades.

The Colonel Roy C. Kirtland Heritage Center is located on the west side also. Doubling as the base's west side visitor's center, the building contains many photographs about Col. Kirtland's life and the missions accomplished by base personnel.

The Samuel Phillips Conference Center contains photographs of the base's research mission, starting with the Special Weapons Command and stretching through the present day. Notably, the center contains General Phillips's uniforms donated by his widow.

Many other historically significant places and items reside around the base property. However, their historical importance is overshadowed by security concerns relating either to the location or the item itself. The significance of these items and places will remain in the hearts and minds of those cleared and able to view them. Perhaps one day, the public will view the whole history of Kirtland through these places.

Air Force chief of staff Gen. David Goldfein (center) is briefed by Chief M.Sgt. Robert Bean, 351st Battlefield Airmen Training Squadron commandant, on October 20, 2017. The 351st personnel unveiled a memorial bronze statue of Airman 1st Class William Pitsenbarger, pararescueman during the Vietnam War and the first enlisted recipient of the Air Force Cross. Pitsenbarger's decoration was later upgraded to the Congressional Medal of Honor in 2000.

Hardin Field on East Kirtland serves as a parade ground, exercise location, and community park. Lt. Gen. Ernest "Moose" Hardin Jr. (1916–1986) enlisted after Pearl Harbor, flew B-17s during World War II, and later participated in the development of the Joint Chiefs of Staff Single Integrated Operations Plan, a new concept of joint operations for nuclear war. He worked for the Department of Energy after retirement until his death. (Author's collection.)

The Bell UH-1F Huey displayed in Rescue Memorial Park commemorates the helicopter used to save 51 lives during the Thompson Canyon flood in Colorado on August 1, 1976. The UH-1F served as a helicopter for search and rescue, missile field security, and special operations beginning in 1964. (Author's collection.)

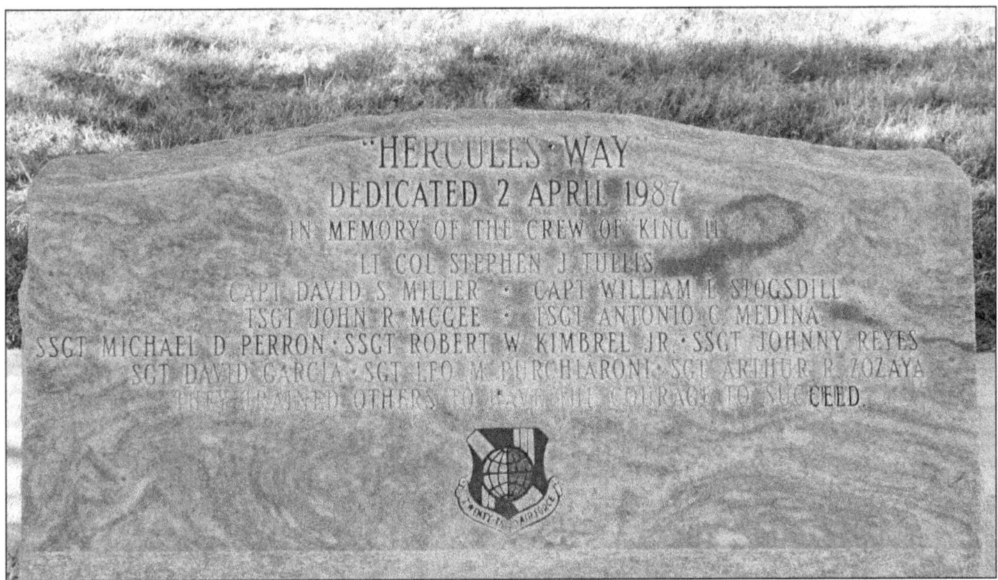

On April 2, 1986, an HC-130 on a routine training mission crashed near Magdalena, New Mexico, killing all 11 crewmembers. The marker remembering the crew of "King 11" was dedicated a year later at Rescue Memorial Park on West Kirtland. (Author's collection.)

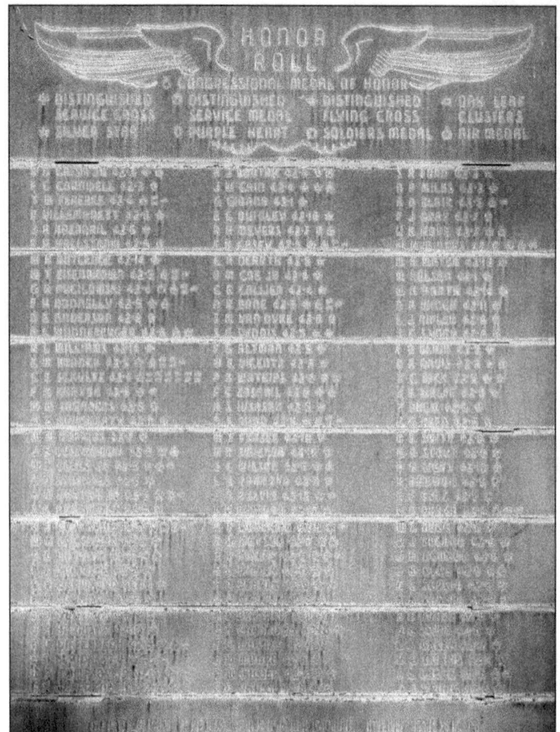

An honor roll near Hardin Field lists aircrew members from Kirtland Field's training classes in 1942. Individual names are listed next to their class number and medals earned during the war. The range of awards listed—Congressional Medal of Honor, Distinguished Flying Cross, Silver Star, Purple Heart, Air Medal—illustrates the hazardous conditions faced by Army Air Force aircrews during World War II. (Author's collection.)

A memorial to the legacy of the base's bombardier training was placed at Hardin Field on the 50th anniversary of World War II. The donating organization, Bombardiers Inc., was dedicated to preserving the legacy of World War II bombardiers. Sadly, with the passing of its founder and a significant number of members, the organization folded in 1996. (Author's collection.)

Located on the west side of Kirtland, Rescue Memorial Park contains airframes and memorial markers from the base's pararescue training mission. The marker recognizes sacrifice that inevitably accompanies the pararescue motto, "These Things We Do, That Others May Live." (Author's collection.)

1ST LT	JOSEPH J MURRAY	JUL	18	1951	COMBAT	F-51
1ST LT	ROBERT J LUCAS	NOV	17	1951	COMBAT	F-51
2D LT	JOHN J BROWNING	SEP	18	1958	TRAINING	F-100
1ST LT	ROUSSEAU J TATMAN JR	DEC	27	1960	TRAINING	F-100
2D LT	DAVID R MCCAULEY	OCT	9	1962	TRAINING	F-100
MAJ	BOBBY G NEELD	JAN	4	1969	COMBAT	F-100
CAPT	MITCHELL S LANE	JAN	4	1969	COMBAT	F-100
CAPT	MICHAEL T ADAMS	MAY	4	1969	COMBAT	F-100
2D LT	JOHN R KELLEY	JUL	8	1972	TRAINING	F-100
1ST LT	SCOTTY W MOSS	MAR	5	1976	TRAINING	A-7
CAPT	JOHN E LACKEY	MAY	1	1978	TRAINING	A-7
CAPT	LAWRENCE A CRONEY	MAY	1	1978	TRAINING	A-7
CAPT	TERRY Q MCCAMMON	OCT	14	1981	TRAINING	A-7
1ST LT	EDDIE J TORREZ	MAY	23	1984	TRAINING	A-7
LT COL	HUGH H WILLIAMS III	JAN	11	1992	TRAINING	A-7
1ST LT	PATRICK J POTTER	APR	22	1998	TRAINING	F-16

This nondescript marker at the 150th Special Operations Wing "Taco Park" lists the fallen unit members from the first fatality in 1951 to the latest in 1998. The list of 5 combat deaths and 11 training deaths are accompanied by the words "Dedicated to the memory of New Mexico Air National Guard pilots who gave their lives in the service of their country." (Author's collection.)

A statue of a soldier kneeling before a battlefield cross is displayed at the New Mexico Veterans' Memorial. While located off the Kirtland military reservation, the Veterans' Memorial contains monuments from all services and wars. Positioned near the Gibson Gate off of Louisiana Boulevard, the Veterans' Memorial hosts events for the public as well as the Kirtland military family, ranging from promotion ceremonies to memorials. (Author's collection.)

Children play at Marquez Park under the watchful gaze of their mother. Lt. Gen. Leo Marquez (1932–2011) was born in Peralta, New Mexico. After earning his pilot's wings, he cross-trained into the aircraft maintenance field, and is considered the "grandfather of Air Force maintenance." Two of his noteworthy achievements include the creation of the Air Force maintenance badge and implementation of the Air Force Combat Ammunitions Center ("Ammo U"). (Author's collection.)

Seven

Aircraft Accidents

A dismal fact of life around military airfields is that planes sometimes crash, and the crew and passengers (and sometimes bystanders) die. Albuquerque has not been immune to this phenomenon. Even though Oxnard and Kirtland Fields focused on aircrew training, there was not a high number of training accidents during World War II. Those that did occur were, however, devestating to the friends and family of the deceased.

After the war, continued training with bombers for the delivery of atomic weapons saw an uptick of accidents involving these special airframes. Four SILVERPLATE B-29s, specially modified for atomic weapons delivery, had accidents at or near Kirtland, two fatal.

Some accidents affected Albuquerque residents directly. On September 11, 1958, during a heavy rainstorm, an F-102 fighter slid off the end of the runway, plowing through a fence and onto Gibson Boulevard. The jet collided with a car driven by Stanley Mendenhall, killing him and his wife, Wallene, instantly.

While a number of aircraft have crashed at Kirtland over the decades, Albuquerque also has the notorious distinction of being the site of two "Broken Arrow" incidents, defined as "an accidental, unauthorized, or unexplained event involving nuclear weapons that could not create the risk of war.

On April 11, 1950, a B-29 aircraft departed Kirtland Air Force Base at 9:38 p.m., and approximately three minutes later crashed into the Manzano foothills, killing the crew. On May 22, 1957, a B-36 aircraft was ferrying a weapon from Biggs Air Force Base, Texas, to Kirtland Air Force Base. At 11:50 a.m., as the aircraft approached Kirtland at an altitude of 1,700 feet, the weapon dropped from the bomb bay, taking the bomb bay doors with it. In both incidents, Department of Defense declassified records state that "a nuclear detonation was not possible."

The first XB-36 rolls out from the Convair plant in 1948. This photograph demonstrates the relative sizes of the B-29 Superfortress and B-36 Peacemaker. These two aircraft types were responsible for Albuquerque's two Broken Arrow nuclear accidents, in 1950 and 1957, respectively. (Courtesy of Air Force Historical Research Agency.)

On April 11, 1950, B-29 s/n 45-21854 crashed into the Manzano foothills, killing all 13 members of the crew. The explosives from the atomic bomb aboard partially detonated, but a nuclear detonation was not possible and no contamination was released. An aluminum plaque was created to mark the site of the first nuclear weapon accident over the continental United States. (Courtesy of the Defense Nuclear Weapons School)

Amateur photographer Allyn "Hap" Hazard filmed the landing of B-36D s/n 49-2660 on May 6, 1951. Moments later, strong crosswinds hit the aircraft, forcing engine number six to hit the runway. The subsequent crash killed 23 of 25 aboard the B-36. Cpl. Richard N. Fogwell and S.Sgt. Jack E. Erickson survived. The high death toll made this the worst air crash in Albuquerque history.

Kirtland fire response crews respond to a F-86 crash on August 1, 1954. The aircraft fuselage is covered in foam fire retardant to prevent any additional fires. (Courtesy of the Air Force Safety Center.)

This map shows the approximate location of the Mark 17 bomb drop site. Due to the low altitude of the drop height, the parachutes did not have time to slow the bomb's descent. Today, little remains of the subsequent crater. The site is approximately two miles from Albuquerque Studios and Mesa Del Sol, a planned living community.

A Mark 17 thermonuclear bomb sits outside of the National Museum of Nuclear Science and History on the east side of Kirtland Air Force Base. Accounts vary on how the 21-ton bomb dropped from the B-36 while on approach to the base. The weapon fell out, taking the aircraft's weapons bay doors with it. The subsequent explosion was described by Air Force officials as "minor," with no property damage.

On April 7, 1961, a pair of F-100As from the New Mexico Air National Guard practiced aerial combat interception techniques with a B-52B from Biggs AFB, Texas. Due to a malfunction, an AIM-9B Sidewinder missile from one F-100A missile destroyed the bomber's left wing, causing it to crash. Four of the seven B-52 crew members survived the ordeal. An accident board cleared the F-100 pilot of any fault.

Ten minutes before midnight on September 14, 1977, an EC-135K s/n 62-3536, similar to the aircraft pictured, crashed into the Manzano foothills on takeoff from Kirtland, killing all 20 occupants. Crash investigators identified crew fatigue as the probable cause, along with extra water weight for the water-injected engines.

In 2017, the Defense Nuclear Weapons School helped the FBI Evidence Recovery Team conduct the first detailed survey of the B-29 crash site in over 68 years to better document the historic site. (Courtesy of the Defense Nuclear Weapons School.)

Three representatives of the American Society of Safety Engineers visit the Air Force Safety Center's crash lab. The lab contains damaged or destroyed hardware ranging from jet engines to F-16 fuselages to rocket stages. Safety students augment their classroom training in mishap investigation with a tour of the outdoor lab in the foothills of the Manzano Mountains.

Eight

Notable Faces at Kirtland

Albuquerque resides at the geographic and cultural crossroads of New Mexico. The creation of Kirtland as an aviation training facility was not only due to clear blue skies and wide-open spaces—connectivity to railroad infrastructure, and later, interstate highways helped boost the movement of people to the area.

As the nearest military installation to New Mexico's largest city, Kirtland is the primary landing location for presidential visits to the Duke City. Since opening in 1941, the base has supported visits from Presidents Kennedy, Nixon, Carter, Reagan, Bush, and Obama, as well as Vice Presidents Johnson and Biden, to name a few. While sightings of Air Force One are not common in New Mexico skies, the close proximity of the Albuquerque International Sunport and Kirtland, along with its shared runways, almost guarantee future presidential visits.

Kirtland has also seen its fair share of celebrities throughout the years, being a hub for aviation training and other national defense research and development. In some cases, such as Jimmy Stewart and Jackie Coogan, their celebrity preceded their military service. For others, fame followed after their time at Kirtland was complete. A subset of others have their claim-to-fame reside in small pockets of history, such as the space program or local history. Regardless of their scope of fame, each one of their stories helps weave the narrative of Kirtland's history.

Known to the entertainment world as "Jimmy," 2nd Lt. James Maitlin Stewart came to Kirtland Field in late 1942. As a twin-engine flight instructor, Stewart would take bombardier students on training flights in AT-11s. By December, he received a transfer to Hobbs Army Airfield for training on the B-17 Flying Fortress. Stewart finished his career in the Air Force Reserves, retiring in 1968 as a brigadier general.

S.Sgt. Jackie Coogan, who was a child star in silent movies, attended the base's Glider Training School in late 1942. Coogan later volunteered for duty with the 1st Air Commando Group in the China Burma India Theater of operations. Coogan returned to Albuquerque in 1945 as part of a War Bond aerial attack demonstration show. He finished his military career as a first lieutenant and returned to Hollywood after the war.

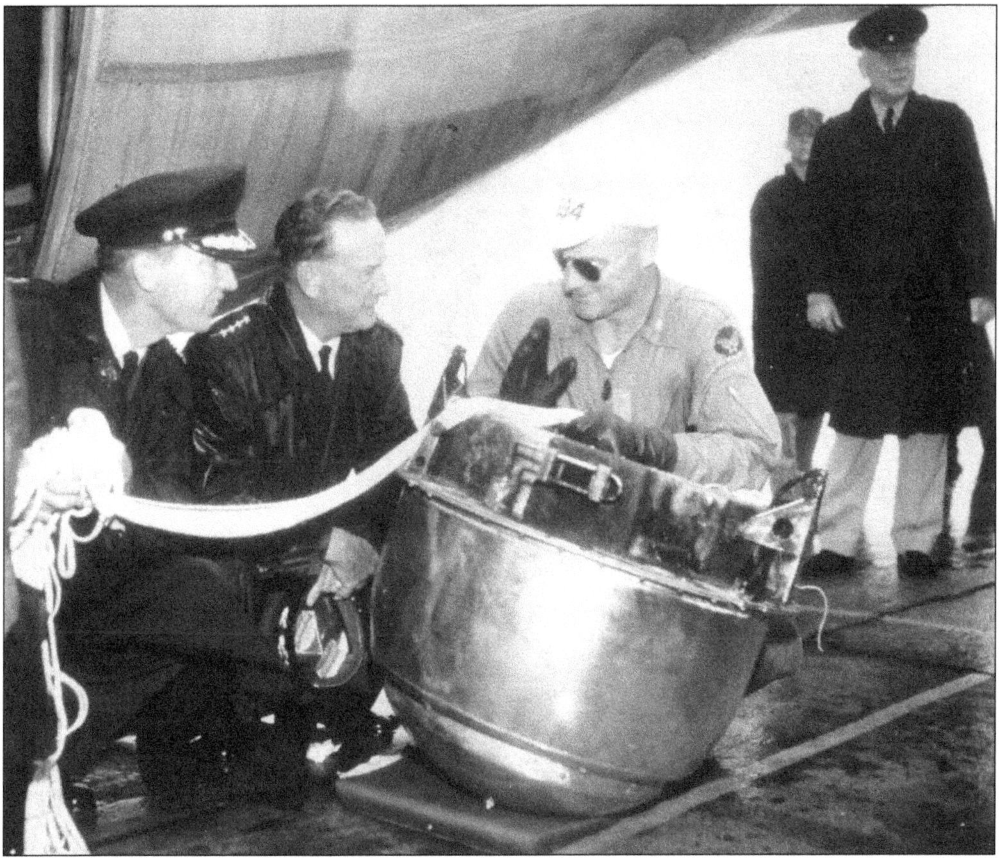

Col. Charles G. "Moose" Mathison (1918–2009), pictured at center wearing a flight suit, presents the Discoverer 13 capsule to Gen. Bernard Schriever (left) and Air Force chief of staff Thomas White (second from left) in August 1960. Mathison was the Kirtland base commander from 1970 to 1972; however, his "hijacking" of the Discoverer 13 capsule in 1960 remains one of the most audacious stories of the National Reconnaissance Program's early days. (Courtesy of the National Reconnaissance Office.)

Selected in the third group for the Manned Orbiting Laboratory program, Maj. Robert H. Lawrence Jr. (1935–1967) was the first African American astronaut in the US space program. Lawrence earned a PhD in chemistry from Ohio State University before being stationed at Kirtland as a research scientist at the Air Force Weapons Laboratory. He was killed during the crash of an F-104 Starfighter at Edwards Air Force Base, California, on December 8, 1967.

Dr. Henry Edward "Ed" Roberts (1941–2010) designed the world's first minicomputer, the Altair 8800. As an active duty Air Force captain, Roberts worked in the Weapons Laboratory's Laser Division along with Forrest Mims. In his spare time, Roberts cofounded Micro Instrumentation and Telemetry Systems (MITS), creating the Altair and directly influencing a little-known software company named Microsoft to come to Albuquerque. (Courtesy of *Make* magazine.)

While deployed to South Vietnam in 1967, 2nd Lt. Forrest Mims III launches a rocket. Mims is the world's most widely read electronics author and is the cofounder of MITS with Ed Roberts. While in Vietnam, Mims's rocketry hobby caught the attention of a colonel who arranged for an engineering assignment at the AFWL's Laser Division. After separating from the service, Mims became a technology writer known for his RadioShack *Engineer's Mini-Notebooks*. (Courtesy of Forrest Mims.)

First Lady Michelle Obama is escorted off Air Force One by a Kirtland military family. The president and first lady arrived in Albuquerque on September 27, 2010, to speak with New Mexico families about improving the economy. During her time as first lady, Obama championed the Joining Forces initiative focused on military members, spouses, and their children.

On December 7, 1962, Pres. John F. Kennedy visited Albuquerque. Landing at Kirtland, he was escorted to the Sandia Corporation's facilities for briefings on atomic research. After staying the night in Albuquerque, President Kennedy traveled to Indian Springs Air Force Auxiliary Field, Nevada, a staging point for above-ground atomic tests and formerly under the administration of the Air Force Special Weapons Center.

Television personality Bill Nye chats with AFRL scientist Jamie Stearns during a visit to the lab in October 2011. As host of the television show *Bill Nye the Science Guy* in the late 1990s, Nye used visual experimentation in scientific principles to encourage children to believe that "Science Rules!" Many current AFRL scientists recall Nye as a motivational force in their careers.

S.Sgt. Christopher Frost of the 377th Air Base Wing Public Affairs Office was the first fatality from Kirtland in Iraq in 2008. In 2011, F Avenue was renamed Frost Avenue in honor of his sacrifice.

S.Sgt. Travis L. Griffin of the 377th Security Forces Squadron died as a result of wounds sustained from an improvised explosive device while on patrol in Baghdad, Iraq, in 2008. In 2012, M Avenue on Kirtland was renamed Griffin Avenue in honor of Staff Sergeant Griffin.

Maj. Steven Plumhoff, an MH-53 pilot from the 58th Operations Squadron, died on November 23, 2003, near Bagram Airfield, Afghanistan. The New Jersey native was participating in Operation Mountain Resolve, supporting operations of the 10th Mountain Division. Plumhoff was highly respected by peers for his ability to perform low-level night flights in dangerous terrain.

The New Mexico sun sets on the American flag at half-staff at Hardin Field on December 7, 2017. Today, Kirtland Air Force Base has evolved into an installation different in many respects from its predecessors: Oxnard Field, Sandia Base, Manzano Base, and Kirtland Field. The scope of its present-day activities could not have been imagined back in 1928, when the old Albuquerque airport first opened for aviation business. (Author's collection.)

Bibliography

Alberts, Don. *Balloons to Bombers: Aviation in Albuquerque: 1882–1945*. Albuquerque, NM: Albuquerque Museum, 1987.

Alberts, Don and Allan Putnam. *A History of Kirtland Air Force Base: 1928–1982*. Albuquerque, NM: 1606th Air Base Wing History Office, 1985.

Doerrfeld, Dean and Rebecca Gatewood. *Air Force Ammunition and Explosives Storage & Unaccompanied Personnel Housing During the Cold War (1946–1989)*. Frederick, MD: R. Christopher Goodwin & Associates Inc., 2008.

Hansen, Chuck. *Swords of Armageddon*. Sunnyvale, CA: Chukelea Publications, 2007.

Hennessy, Juliette. *The United States Army Air Arm: April 1861 to April 1917*. Washington, DC: Office of Air Force History, 1985.

Little, R.D. *History of the Air Force Participation in the Atomic Energy Program, 1943–1953*. Maxwell AFB, AL: Air University Historical Liaison Office, 1953.

Loeber, Charles R. *Building the Bombs: A History of the Nuclear Weapons Complex (Second Edition)*. Albuquerque, NM: Sandia National Laboratories, 2002.

Moyers, James "Al." "Team Kirtland: A Brief History of Kirtland AFB." Powerpoint Presentation. Kirtland AFB, NM: Air Force Nuclear Weapons Center Office of History, 2016.

Reynolds, Kristen. *Wings of War: An Illustrated History of Kirtland Air Force Base, 1941–1960*. Albuquerque, NM: 377th Air Base Wing, 2016.

Taylor, Leland. *History of Air Force Atomic Cloud Sampling*. Kirtland AFB, NM: Air Force Special Weapons Center Office of Information, 1963.

Thompson, Matt. *70 Years of Training & Education: A History of the Defense Nuclear Weapons School 1947–2017*. Unpublished master's thesis. Charlestown, WV: American Public University System, 2016.

Van Citters, Karen and Kristen Bisson. *National Register of Historic Places Historic Context and Evaluation for Kirtland Air Force Base*. Albuquerque, NM: Van Citters Historic Preservation LLC, 2003.

Van Citters, Karen and Deborah Butcher. *Documentation of the TRESTLE at Kirtland Air Force Base, New Mexico*. Albuquerque, NM: Van Citters Historic Preservation LLC, 2003.

Watson, Stephen F. "From 'Splendid Aviator' to 'Capable Executive:' Colonel Roy C. Kirtland and the Development of Army Aviation." Unpublished article.

www.ingramcontent.com/pod-product-compliance
Lightning Source LLC
LaVergne TN
LVHW081545100826
845153LV00004B/315

* 9 7 8 1 5 4 0 2 3 5 1 1 4 *